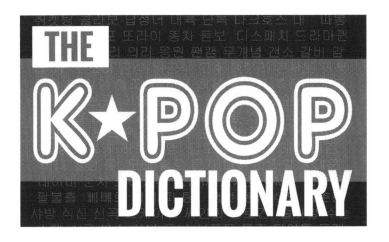

THE K★POP DICTIONARY

FULLY UNDERSTAND WHAT YOUR FAVORITE IDOLS ARE SAYING

BY WOOSUNG KANG

N€ D1468809

"The Kpop Dictionary is a fun mix of common slang and adages frequently found in Kpop and Korean Dramas which will help provide a base for understanding that goes far beyond subtitles. As a YouTube personality who focuses on the ever-changing world of Korean entertainment, I see this book being an extremely useful resource to anyone interested in improving their comprehension of Korean Dramas and Kpop."

- Stephanie Ishler, Hallyu Back -

THE KPOP DICTIONARY

A dictionary of honest human interaction,
Korean pop culture, and everyday K-POP
life. A resource for language learners
confused by real-world Korean, and a
tool to help you understand the world of
a K-POP fan. But more importantly, great
entertainment for everyone.

Introduction

Hello, K-Pop fan! Congratulations on your bold decision to embark on a journey to the fantastic world of K-Pop! Let's take a moment to share the joy: you have chosen your favorite *bias*, you can tell who is the *maknae* of the group, right? Oh, and you must know who is in charge of the *visual* and has the best *aegyo* that melts your heart!

Well, it's okay if you don't have a clue about what I just said, because that is probably the reason you chose to read this book. It is designed it so you can learn the most up-to-date vocabulary that is used in K-POP lyrics, TV shows, K-Dramas and the like.

As the title of this book suggests, this is not an ordinary dictionary. It is specifically designed to explain what these words mean in a K-Pop and K-Drama context. These are like encrypted codes that can only be understood if you know the background information, such as where they originated, and when and how they are used. Without this knowledge, you are missing out on all the news and updates other fans are talking about!

For that reason, this book also includes real life examples of the words in action. You will gain a thorough understanding of the words and their background information. So you can use this book as a quick reference guide any time you run into K-Pop and K-Drama lingo, or as a study reference by utilizing the conversation examples included on every page. Whatever your goal, this will be a great way to expand your K-Pop and K-Drama knowledge, and to give yourself a window into the fascinating world of Korean culture!

You will notice that sometimes there are more than one spelling variations. Despite the fact that there is a standard method of Romanizing Korean words using Latin letters, K-Pop fans and translators have chosen to haphazardly use whatever they think is appropriate. Those Romanizations have then spread across the Internet, eventually becoming the new standards used by everyone. So, this book includes the versions that are popularly used among K-Pop fans, but spellings in Hangeul (Korean alphabet) are also provided - you can always cross-check in case you want clarification and further detail.

Hang Syo!

5-Year Curse

Noun. "Jinx Whereby Popular Groups Will Face Hardships or Disbandment in Their Fifth Year"

Many Fans of KPOP superstitiously believe there's a reason why popular groups like H.O.T., Big Bang, TVXQ, Shinhwa, Super Junior have experienced bad luck over the past five years. On the other hand, others have shrugged it off as pure coincidence. They believe people have a habit of taking ordinary events and turning them into curses!

Example)
Tomi : Breaking news, guys! Cutie 5 just broke up!
Yena: Oh no, the *5-year curse* is true… they debuted exactly 5 years ago!

아닥 A Dak
(a-dak)

Phrase. "Shut Your Pie Hole"

An abbreviation for "아가리" *ah ga ri* (vulgar term for "mouth") "닥쳐" *dak chyeo* ("shut up"). These are fighting words, but in an abbreviated form, these same expressions are used among friends and seen as just great fun. The abbreviations seem to tone down the meaning so they come across as cute!

Example)
Uncle Jay: Dude! Do you know why 10 is afraid of 7?
Max: Um… no?
Uncle Jay: Cause seven eight (ate) nine!
Max: That is such an *ajae gag*…

아점 A Jeom
(a-jŏm)

Noun. "Brunch"

A compound word made up of "아침" *achim* ("breakfast") + "점심" *jeom shim* ("lunch") = "brunch". Some people have an interesting way of distinguishing one from other. If a meal is average, it is "아점", but if a meal is worthy of Instagram, then it's brunch. This is largely due to some

Korean people's tendency to associate imported English words with style.

Example)
Taeho: Hey baby, let's go get achim!
Minji: Wha... achim? It's already 11:30AM!
Taeho: Well then, jeom shim it is!
Minji: More like *ajeom*, right?
Taeho: Maybe, depends on what we are having.
Minji: I don't know... maybe eggs benedict with mimosa?
Taeho: It is brunch then!

아놔 A Nwa
(a-nwa)

Interjection. "What the..."
Something that automatically comes out of your mouth when you are
irritated or angry. It is actually the first part of the exclamation (e.g., "아놔"
a nwa "정말" *jeong mal* ("really") "화난다" *hwa nan da* ("I am angry")
while leaving out the rest of the phrase. This will send a much clearer
message.

Example)
Sohee: Hon, you should come see this...!
Kai: What's up?
Sohee: I accidentally unplugged your computer...
Kai: *A Nwa*

아템 A Tem
(a-t'em)

Noun. "Item"
The way kids and teens speak, especially during Internet game play.

Example)
Mingoo: Attack! Attack! Destroy this hideous monster!
Mingoo's game character defeats the monster.
Jiwon: Dang! You did it! Did you get any *atem*?
Mingoo: Hells yeah! I got this holy shield as a reward!

애빼시 Ae Bbae Si
(ae-ppae-shi)

Phrase. "Full of Aegyo"

An abbreviation for "애교" *aegyo* ("acting cutesy") + "빼면" *bbae myeon* ("if wihout") + "시체" *shi che* ("corpse")". Meaning, "Without aegyo, a person is a corpse" = "A person is nothing but aegyo".

Example)
Wonmi: Darling~ my love~ <3 <3 <3
Hojoon: LOL! Why are you so full of *aegyo* today?
Wonmi: Not just today~ everyday *^_^*
Hojoon: Yup, that's why people call you *ae bbae si*!

애인 Ae In
(ae-in)

Noun. "Lover"

A compound word made up of two Chinese words "애" *ae* ("love") + "인" *in* ("person")". The best way to distinguish "애인" from a boyfriend/ girlfriend is to remember that a boyfriend/girlfriend can be a lover, but a lover is NOT necessarily a boyfriend/girlfriend.

Example)
Hye: Sweetheart, am I your girlfriend?
Cheolsoo: Not… really.
Hye: WTF? What am I to you then?
Cheolsoo: (In panic) Um… you are my *ae in*! My lover!
Hye: Ok… so you have someone else as your girlfriend?
Cheolsoo: I want my lawyer.

애자 Ae Ja
(ae-ja)

Noun. "Crippled"

A derogatory way of saying "장애자" *jang ae ja* ("a person with a disability")". It is often used among teenagers as a way of ridiculing someone who performs poorly in competitive games, or someone who can't keep up with the activities of others. Due to the sensitive nature of the word, it should not be used outside a group of friends.

Example)
Mark: Dude, come on! Our base is under attack!
Tim: Yeah man, I am doing my best but can't remember how to… attack the enemies…FML.
Mark: Are you *ae ja*? I told you over 100 times!

애교 Aegyo
(ae-gyo)

Noun. "Acting Cutesy"
A compound word made up of two Chinese characters where "ae" means "love" and "gyo" means "beautiful". It is a display of affection through various expressions such as making cute gestures or speaking in baby talk. While strongly associated with feminine traits, male KPOP idols often display these affections, but it is not frowned upon.

Example)
Yuna: Oppa~! Can I pweeeeease have a hug~? (Baby voice)
Minho: Of course, but only if you do the cutie dance!
Yuna starts dancing like a 5-year-old girl
Minho: Your *aegyo* really melts me! <3 <3

애교살 Aegyo Sal
(ae-gyo-sal)

Noun. "Lower Part of the Eyelid"
A word that refers to the lower eyelid; not to be confused with eye bags which sits below "aegyo sal" and give you a hung-over zombie look. Fuller "aegyo sal" is commonly achieved through plastic surgery, and is usually performed by injecting one's own abdominal fat, or a commercial filler. The belief is that having fuller "aegyo sal" makes eyes look bigger and youthful.

Example)
Jenny: Hey girl, your eyes look different, what happened?

Tina: Can you tell? I just got my *aegyo sal* injected at Dr. Kim's office.
Jenny: Oh, that's sweet! You do look younger. Will I get the same result if I drink 5 glasses of wine and have an all-nighter tonight?
Tina: Haha you can try but I am sure it will only get you puffy eyes!

Age Line

Noun. "Group of People Born in the Same Year"
The term "line" can be translated as "grouping" or "belonging", and when combined with the term "age", it means a group of people who were born in the same year. It is always grouped by the last two digits of the year, rather than their age.

Example)
Tammy, Yohan, and Juno are from the 93-line (o)
Tammy, Yohan, and Juno are from the 23 year old-line (x)
Ara: Nice to meet you all! My name is Ara, and was born in 1994. Oh, my blood type is AB.
Yumi, Jihun, and Tony: Welcome to the 94-*line*!

아이구 Aigoo (Aigo)
(a-i-gu)

Interjection. "Oops"
An expression used to show frustration, embarrassment, and surprise. English equivalents are "aw man" and "oops". It is also used when scolding somebody.

Example)
Aigoo! I forgot to do my homework!
Aigoo, I have no money in my wallet.
Did you break this vase? *Aigoo*, you clumsy little bastard!

아재 Ajae
(a-jae)

Noun. `"Someone/Something Outdated"`

A Gangwon province dialect for "아저씨" ajuhssi ("uncle"), "middle-aged man" or "married man", but can be used to address an unfamiliar adult male. It is often translated as "mister" in English. Recently, this word has been associated with someone who is very archaic or old-fashioned.

Example)
Goyoung: What did one plate say to the other? Lunch is on me! LOL!
Bo: *Ajae* please…

아재 개그 Ajae Gag
(a-jae-gae-gǔ)

Noun., Adjective. `"Dad Jokes"`

A compound word made up of "아재" *ajae* ("outdated") + "개그" *gag* ("jokes"). When used, it does not bring about laughter but an awkward moment of silence. It is not only ajaes that make lame jokes, though. Regardless of age, if someone is not up on the latest trends and tells old, tired jokes, they are an ajae.

Example)
Making *ajae gag* adds at least 20 years to your actual age.

아줌마 Ajumma (Ajoomma)
(a-jum-ma)

Noun. `"Married or Middle-aged Woman"`

A word for a "married or middle-aged woman" which is often translated as "madam" in English, but when used in certain situations, its nuance is subtly different. For example, if a young, unmarried woman behaves badly, calling her "ajumma" becomes an insult. This is because there are negative connotations associated with the word, such as being pushy, loud, and sometimes selfish. The most distinctive characteristic of this word is a women with permed hair, similar to that of a grandmother's. Some people believe that "ajumma" is the third gender in Korea. It can also be used to address a restaurant waitress.

Example)
Wow, that *ajumma* literally stole that old man's seat!
Did you hear that? Jenny became so *ajumma* after having 2 kids!
That super-curly perm she got makes her look like a total *ajumma!*
Ajumma! Can we please have another pair of chopsticks?

아저씨 Ajusshi (Ahjussi)
(a-jŏ-ssi)

Noun "Married or Middle-aged Man"
The male counterpart of "ajumma". This is a word for a "middle-aged man" or "married man" but can be used to address an unfamiliar adult male. It is often translated as "mister" in English. While similar to "ajumma", there are less negative connotations associated with it. The biggest insult would be calling a young man "ajusshi", because that means he is old-fashioned or outdated.

Example)
Oppa! That joke is so outdated… So *ajusshi*!

Ashley: Ajusshi! Can you tell me the directions to Seoul?"
Kyuwon: Um… okay…, but FYI, I am not ajusshi.

악플 Ak Peul
(ak-p'ŭl)

Noun. "Malicious Comments" or "Cyber Bulling".
A compound word made up of "악" *ak* ("evi"l) "플" *peul* ("reply/comment"). This has been a huge problem in Korea because of cases where celebrities have committed suicide after being cyber bullied on the Internet. This is also a tactic used by certain fan clubs during "fan wars"

Example)
Mira: Wow! I have over 200 comments on my selfie I posted last night.
Hailey: Um… did you read any of them?

Mira: Yeah… they are all *ak peul*'s… but I got over 200 comments! Yes I am popular!

Hailey: Not sure if you are too dumb or just too optimistic…

알바 Alba (Arba)
(al-ba)

Noun. "Part Time Job"

A shortened phrase for "arbeit", which is a German word for "to labor", but has been used to mean "part time job" in Korea.

Example)

Sangmi: What are you doing this Friday night?

Taeho: I have to arba at seven eleven until 11 PM.

Sangmi: Oh no, how many *arba*'s are you doing?

Taeho: Four, cause I need money to buy my idol Oppa's gifts!

올킬 All-kill
(ol-k'il)

Noun. Winning All Major Music Download Sites"

A word used to describe an artist or a group topping all major music download sites (i.e., Melon, Soribada, Dosirak, etc.), it is said to be an "all-kill", since it is "killing all the charts". It is relatively easy to achieve an all-kill in the daily charts, but weekly or monthly charts are more difficult.

Example)

Yay! Our Oppa's new single *all-killed* the charts!

안무 An Moo
(an-mu)

Noun. "Choreography"

One of many essential elements (i.e., good "visual", friendly fan service, etc.) that an idol group must have in order to make an album successful. It is designed to complement the "concept" of their album (e.g., "sexy", "innocent", or "strong"). Some of the notable examples are "Tell Me

Dance" by Wonder Girls and "In-line 5-Cylinder Engine Dance" by Crayon Pop. An Moo is an extremely important factor that determines the success of an album because well-designed dance moves alone can make a song go viral.

Example)
Mina: OMG! Did you see Biggie Biggie's new *an moo*? The dance moves are so sexy!
Yesol: I can't wait to see!

안물안궁 An Mool An Goong
(an-mu-ran-'gung)

Phrase. "I Did Not Ask and I Am Not Curious, Either."
An abbreviation for "안 물어봄" *an mool eo bom* ("I didn't ask"), "안 궁금함" *an goong geum ham* ("I am not curious"). This is what you say to stop someone who frequently pours out unsolicited information.

Example)
Jinsoo: So I woke up today at 7AM, and had 2 cups of coffee, and hit the gym at 9AM, right? After that I took a shower for 20 minutes, got dressed up, and went to work. Oh, and I had Chinese for lunch!
Yoosun: *An mool an goong…* you can stop now.

안습 An Seup
(an-sŭp)

Noun. "Pathetic Situation"
An abbreviation for "안구에" *an goo e* ("in the eyes") + "습기" *seup gi* ("moisture") = "moist eyes". It is your body's natural reaction to strong, emotional events, such as your "bias" going into the army or failing to top the music charts.

Example)
Hyomin: Oh no! LOL!
Wonkyu: What's up?
Hyomin: Alex was performing on the stage at this girls' high school, and he just tripped, his shoe came off, and the best part is, his sock had a huge hole in it. All the girls there must have seen it.

Wonkyu: LOL! That is really *an seup*...

안드로메다 Andromeda
(an-dŭ-ro-me-da)

Noun. `"Out of One's Mind"`

Literally meaning "sending someone's common sense to the Andromeda Galaxy", it refers to someone who does not have the ability to make good judgment calls or who is not able to behave in a practical and sensible way. It is a popular phrase among the younger generation.

Example)
Caleb: LOL! I just farted in my girlfriend's face!
Miha: OMG. Did you send your brain to the *Andromeda* or something?

안돼 Andwae
(an-dwae)

Interjection. `"You Can't", "Can't Be Done"`

Literally meaning "no, you can't", or "it can't be done", it is often used as a way to express disbelief, amazement, fear, shock, or defiance, having the same effect as saying "no way!".

Example)
Sohyun: Oppa, can I please have one more shot of Soju?
Minki: Andwae.
Tina: Oh my god! News broke out that your favorite Idol group XOXO's member has been secretly dating that back dancer girl.
Minyoung: *Andwae*!

Antis

Noun. `"Anti-someone"`

A shortened phrase for "anti-someone". A person or a group of people who show hatred toward a certain artist or a group; mainly because of an ongoing rivalry between the artists or a group they like. Some would go as far as sabotaging their rival's concerts or sending threatening packages like knives, blood-covered dolls, etc.

Example)
JAJA has so many *antis*, especially from the ABAB fan club. I am pretty
sure it's because JAJA crushed them by all-killing the chart when their new
song came out the same time theirs did. ABAB's sales was just lackluster.

아파 Apa
(a-pa)

Noun. "It Hurts", "Name of the Song by"
Name of the song by 2NE1, which translates to "it hurts".

Example)
Felix: *Apa!*
Mihyun: You hurt?
Felix: Lol, nope. I'm just listening to 2NE1.

군대 Army (Goon Dae)
(gun-dae)

Noun. "Mandatory Military Service for Korean Males"
Refers to mandatory military service which all able-bodied males over the
age of 20 have to go through. The duration of the service is 21 months for
the army, and 23 months for the navy and the air force. Any male idols who
are in the military can't engage in commercial activities such as appearing
on TV or performing at concerts.

Example)
Jay Juno, the leader of group POPO just received notice of enlistment. He
will be in the *army* for next 2 years! I wonder how his group will survive
without him.

ASKY

Phrase. "Not Happening"
An abbreviation for "안" *an* ("not") "생겨요" *saeng gye yo* ("~ is
happening"). It is a self-derogatory expression used as an answer to the
heart rendering question: "Do you have a boyfriend/girlfriend?"
Example)

Nina: Merry Christmas to myself…!
Joe: Hey, why are you alone on Christmas? Where is your date?
Nina: *ASKY…*

아싸 Assa
(a-ssa)

Interjection. "Oh Yes!"
An expression that automatically comes out of your mouth when something is in your favor, such as your favorite idol group winning the Dae Sang at the Golden Disk Awards.

Example)
(Marcus and Taeho playing poker)
Marcus: *Assa!* I got full house, homes! Gimme your money!
Taeho: Not so fast! I got royal straight flush! Assa! I win!

바보 Babo
(ba-bo)

Noun "Idiot", "Silly"
Not an extremely derogatory term compared to other possible alternatives, and is often used in friendly settings as well.

Example)
Mihyun: Oppa! Do you know what tomorrow is?
Ohwi: I dunno, Monday?
Mihyun: You are such a *babo!* It's our one-year anniversary!
Ohwi: Aigoo.

배고파 Bae Go Pa
(bae-go-p'a)

Phrase. "I'm Hungry"
The term "배" bae means "stomach", and "고파" gopa means "hungry". Hence, if you insert a different term in place of "배", it means "something hungry = hungry for something (i.e., 사랑 *sarang* 고파 *gopa* = "love

hungry").

Example)
Girlfriend: *Bae Go Pa!*
Boyfriend: What do you want to eat?
Girlfriend: I dunno… maybe Mexican food?
Boyfriend: Ok then let's go get some Burritos.
Girlfriend: I dunno… maybe Chinese?
Boyfriend: O…Kay, let's go to that Dim Sum place.
Girlfriend: I dunno… maybe I am not hungry?
Boyfriend: WTH? What do you *really* want?
Girlfriend: Now I am upset.

배우 Baewoo
(bae-u)

Noun "Actor"
For a female actress, it is "여*(yeo)baewoo*", as "yeo" means "female".

Example)
Inbi is a great singer but she would have made a good *yeobaewoo* if she chose that path.

베이글 녀/남
Bagel Girl (Nyeo)/Boy (Nam)
(be-i-gŭl nyŏ/nam)

Noun "Someone Who Has a Baby Face With An Amazing Body"
For female idols, "bagel" is a compound word made up of "(ba)by face" and "(gl)amorous", thus pronounced as "bagel". Here, "glamorous" is used to mean "voluptuous". This is a term exclusively used for female idols who have a younger-looking face and a voluptuous body. For male idols, "glamorous" is changed to "gladiator".

Example)
Hyuni's such a *bagel neyo* – she has the face of a high school girl and the body of a pin-up girl.

I never knew Wonki had such a great body because of his baby face. He is a great example of a *bagel nam*.

발연기 | Bal Yeon Gi
(bal-lyŏn-'gi)

Noun. "Sloppy Acting"
Literally means "acting with foot", because the word "발" *bal* ("foot") is used as a prefix to refer to something of low quality. In the Korean entertainment industry, many idols want to break into acting, because it exposes them to greater opportunities like getting a CF. While many idols have made the transition successfully, many have delivered lackluster performances. A good example is Jang Soo-won, a former Sechs Kes idol who earned the nickname "Robot Actor" for his poor acting abilities.

Example)
Ura: Did you see the new drama last night? Ugh… I couldn't stand a moment watching our oppa doing *bal yeon gi*…
Miyo: I know… (sigh) Maybe our oppa should just stick to singing.

발라드 Ballad
(bal-la-dŭ)

Noun "Sentimental and Emotional Song About Love"
One of the most popular KPOP genres which remains a constant in the music charts. Ballad singers are thought to have better singing skills than "dance groups". This is why the members of idol groups, who have great singing skills, choose this genre when they go solo and need an "image makeover".

Example)
When Semin sings a *ballad* song, his fangirls drown themselves in tears.

반대 Ban Dae
(ban-dae)

Noun. "Objection"

A term you should familiarize yourself with if you are an avid fan of K-Drama. In Korea, a couple wanting to marry must first seek approval from the parents of both families. However, (in order to make it more dramatic), there's always someone who doesn't like the idea. Some of the reasons are 1) He/she does not come from a wealthy family or 2) The couple is actually brother and sister, separated at birth.

Example)
Minki: Mom, dad, please allow us to get married!
Mom: I don't know. What do you think, honey?
Dad: *Ban Dae!*
Minki: But dad, why?
Dad: Her personality is so similar to your mom's, and I don't want to see you suffer like I did.

반도 Ban Do
(ban-do)

Noun. "Korea"

An Internet term mostly used by the younger generation of netizens. "한반도" *han ban do* literally means "The Korean Peninsula" and "*ban do*" alone means "Peninsula". Since there aren't very many countries that are peninsulas, netizens simply use it to refer to Korea. It is most frequently used in the form of "반도의" *ban do eui* ~sth = "sth of Korea". For example, "반도의 패션 (fashion)" is "Fashion of Korea".

Example)
Wayne: Dude, what is that thing you eating?
Brian: It's Kimchi! *Bando*'s staple food!

반모 Ban Mo
(ban-mo)

Noun. "Talking/Speaking in an Informal Way".
An abbreviation for "반말 모드" *ban mal* ("informal way of speaking") mode. This occurs either through an implicit mutual agreement (because participants are of a similar age or they have developed a certain level of closeness) or by permission (usually the older participant initiates this and lets the younger follow suit).
Example)
Doori: Hello Mr. Kim, how is your day going?
Hoon: What's with all the formality man? We are both in the 5th grade! Let's go *ban mo*, buddy!
Doori: Aight dude!

바나나우유 Banana Milk (Woo Yoo)
(ba-na-na-u-yu)

Noun. "Banana Flavored Milk"
A delicious Korean banana-flavored milk that became very famous overseas thanks to a popular commercial featuring Lee Min Ho.

Example)
Mmm, this *banana milk* is so delicious! It's amazing that it contains no real banana!

반말 Banmal
(ban-mal)

Noun. "Informal Way of Speaking"
Literally meaning "half-words", it is an informal (talking down) way of speaking. It should only be used by those close to you or younger than you. It is extremely rude when used toward someone older than you, or before a close friendship has been established. Foreigners who are unfamiliar with the Korean language are mostly forgiven for making such mistakes.

Example)
Wow, before I got better at Korean, I used to talk to my professor in *banmal*. Now I feel so embarrassed! Ignorance is bliss.

밥 Bap
(bap)

Noun. "Meal" or "Punching Bag"
Literal meaning is a "meal", or a "bowl of rice", but is figuratively used to refer to someone who is looked down on as an easy prey ("easy meal").

Example)
Min: Hey, you wanna play Starcraft? 1:1?
Tony: Again? I can beat you with my eyes blindfolded. You are my *bap*!

뻘글 Bbeol Geul
(ppŏl-gŭl)

Noun. "Useless/Meaningless Post"
"뻘" *bbeol* means "useless" and "meaningless" in Korean dialect and "글" *geul* means "a writing/post". Newly registered users on Internet forums often write these in order to reach a certain level/membership (e.g., rookie, junior, senior, contributor, and etc.) which is granted after meeting a certain threshold (e.g., 20 posts).

Example)
Joann: What are you doing?
Max: I'm busy writing bunch of meaningless *bbeol geul*'s.
Joann: For what?
Max: This stupid forum says I have to make 20 posts to be able to read other's posts.

뻥 Bbeong
(ppŏng)

Noun. Interjection. "Bull" "Lie" "Fib" "Hot Air"
An adjective used to describe the popping sound of an object (e.g., a balloon), but it is colloquially used to refer to somethingthat is not true or overly exaggerated.

Example)
Alexander: Dude! You just got a letter from the FBI!
Victor: WTF? What does it say?
Alexander: OMG… What did you do man…
Victor: Why? Just tell me already!
Alexander: It says… *"Bbeong!"*
Victor: I will kill you one day…

뽀대 Bbo Dae
(ppo-dae)

Noun. "Swag".
Synonymous with "간지" *ganji* ("fashionable"), and can be used interchangeably.

Example)
Dongyu: Look at my new ride!
Nathan: Is that a Ferrari?
Dongyu: Hell yeah!
Nathan: It's full of *bbo dae*.

뽐뿌 Bbom Bbu
(ppom-ppu)

Noun. "Encourage", "Incite", "Egg On"
Originated from the English word "pump", when someone becomes overly excited and becomes "all pumped up" often as a result of a compliment or comment. This tactic is especially effective when the person is incapable of making clear judgments (e.g., intoxicated).

Example)
Bongmin: Ok, which one should I get? Red or Blue?
Tina: They both look great on you! Get them both! Oh, this white one also looks terrific on you. Hm, you should also get this pair of shoes!
Bongmin: Stop… *Bbom Bbuing* me…

뿌잉뿌잉 Bbuing Bbuing
(ppu-ing ppu-ing)

Noun. "Something You Say to Look Cute"
A word describing the act of someone (usually girls) employing a cute (aegyo) behavior in an attempt to display their charm. The behavior involves putting up two fists next to cheeks and making a circular motion while saying the term "bbuing bbuing" in a baby voice.

Example)
Sonya: Oppa are you mad? *Bbuing Bbuing~*
Tony: Oh, not any more.

베프 Be Peu
(be-p'ŭ)

Noun. "Best Friend"
An abbreviation "Best Priend" (because there is no F sound in Korean). It describes someone who is willing to go the extra mile and gladly make sacrifices for another, but sometimes, by a quirk of fate, makes your 베프 into an arch-nemesis.

Example)
Jayna: Hey, it's official. We are not friends anymore.
Song: What do you mean? Did I do something wrong?
Jayna: No, we are *Be Peu*'s from now on!
Song: Oh my! Best Friends Forever!

베플 Be Peul
(be-p'ŭl)

Noun. **"Best Reply (Comment)"**

An abbreviation for "베스트" best "리플" *ripeul* (reply/comment). It refers to the top-rated comment on a certain (e.g., Facebook) post. On Facebook, for example, it is the comment with the most number of likes received. For some, it means a lot and can serve as a self-esteem booster.

Example)
Adam: Wow! I left a funny comment on K-Dragon's photo and it became *be peul*! I have over 500 likes so far.
Ignacio: What did you write?
Adam: I said that if I get over 100 likes, I would post a photo of me in a bikini.
Ignacio: You should keep your word.

버카충 Beo Ca Choong
(bŏ-k'a-ch'ung)

Noun. **"Reloading Bus Card's Balance"**

An abbreviation popularly used by teenagers for "버스 카드 충전" bus card choong jeon ("reload/recharge"). In Korea, public transportation has a dedicated terminal that accepts a prepaid card (T-Money). Its balance requires constant reloading to avoid uninterrupted use.

Example)
Min: Damn, I need to get *beo ca choong* before getting on the bus.
Glen: It's all used up already?
Min: Yeah, I shouldn't have let my little brother use it.

버정 Beo Jeong
(bŏ-jŏng)

Noun. "Bus Stop"
An abbreviation for "버스 정거장" bus *jeong geo jang* ("station"). In
K-Dramas, this is where the main character falls in love with a total
stranger, while waiting for a bus, but it is also the place where they say
good-bye to each other.

Example)
Jackie: I'm getting of at this *beo jeong.*
Wendy: Okay girl, hit me up when you get home! I'm getting off at the next
beo jeong.

브금 Beu Geum
(bŭ-gŭm)

Noun. "Back Ground Music (BGM)"
BGM spelled the way it sounds. It is one of the most important elements
of a movie, drama, and variety TV show as it sets the mood, emotion, and
also adds a dramatic effect. Not to be confused with Original Sound Track
(OST), which is the compilation of all individual songs (instrumental,
karaoke, ED, BGM) used in the work. BGM is music used as a background
piece.

Example)
Julie: Oh I can't believe my favorite drama is over.
Ashley: Me neither *crying*. It was part of my life. The *beu geum* is still
stuck in my head!

비친 Bi Chin
(bi-ch'in)

Noun. "Friend Who Keeps Your Secrets"
An abbreviation for "비밀" *bimil* ("secret") "지켜주는" *jikyeo joo neun*
("keeping") "친구" chingoo ("friend"). It refers to someone to whom you
can openly tell your most serious concerns, without worrying about hearing

it through someone else later on.

Example)
Yumi: Can I tell you a secret?
Pamela: Of course! I thought we were *bi chin*? Your secret is safe with me.
Yumi: I just won the lottery!
Pamela: Hey guys! OMG! Yumi won the lottery! Hold her tight so she can't run away!

비추 Bi Choo
(bi-ch'u)

Noun. "Not Recommended"
The opposite of "강추" *gang choo*. The word "비" *bi* is a Chinese word for "no(n)".

Example)
Joe: What do you think about this hat?
Yong: *Bi choo…* Snapbacks are so yesterday…

비담 Bi Dam
(bi-dam)

Noun. "The Best Looking Member of a Group"
A compound word made up of "비쥬얼" *visual* "담당" *dam dang* ("someone in charge of something") = someone in charge of "*visual*".

Example)
Annie: Ok girls, welcome to the first meeting of the book club. We have 6 members total… and you! What is your name?
Jenny: Jenny.
Annie: Ok, since you are pretty, you will be the *vi dam*!
Jenny: Do we really need that for a book club…

Bias

Noun. "Your Favorite Idol"
Your absolute favorite singer or group whom you will support no matter what, hence the term.

Example)
Infinion is my *bias!* I love my Oppa's so much!

Bias Ruiner

Noun. "Someone Who Has the Potential of Becoming Your New Favorite"
An idol singer, an actor, or a group who threatens to take over the place in your heart currently occupied by your current bias.

Example)
Tiffany: OMG, who is that cute boy full of swag?
Minhee: Oh, that is Taemin, the leader of a new idol group named GOGO
Tiffany: Holy moly Guacamole! I thought Seho Oppa was my one and only love but he's so hot that he has the potential to be a *bias ruiner*.

Big 3

Noun. "The Three Major Entertainment Companies in the KPOP Industry"
The nickname for the three major entertainment companies in the KPOP industry in Korea. They are JYP Entertainment, SM Entertainment, and YG Entertainment.

Example)
Kisoo just signed a contract with YG Entertainment. He started his career as a trainee at JYP Entertainment, and debuted through SM Entertainment, and now he is with YG Entertainment! He has gone through all *Big 3*!

블랙데이 Black Day

Noun. "Singles' Day"
Unofficial, more of a tongue-in-cheek day of consolation, observed each year on April 14th by singles in Korea. It is related to Valentine's Day and White Day—on these days, people who have not received gifts gather together wearing black and eat black-colored food, such as "짜장면" *Jjajangmyeon* (a Korean-Chinese noodle dish made with a thick black bean sauce), as a means of sympathizing with each other.

Example)
Hong: Yo~ what you doing tomorrow?
Mogi: Um… It's *black day*… so I guess eat Jjajangmyeon with you?
Hong: Singles rule!!! (cries)

블랙오션 Black Ocean

Noun. "Fans Boycotting a Performance"
A form of protest where fans in the audience dress in all black and do not use light sticks, thereby creating complete darkness.

Example)
After the incident, the idol group ILLO decided to kick out their member Yoon. Fans who are against the decision protested by creating a *black ocean* at ILLO's live performance on TV.

Body Rolls

Noun. "Sexy Dance Move"
A seductive dance move by either male or female KPOP idols. The most popular example is doing the "body wave dance". The slower it is performed the sexier it is perceived!

Example)
Wanso is so flexible that her *body rolls* remind me of the great Tsunami! I bet I can go surfing on it.

보고싶어 Bogoshipo
(bo-go-shi-p'ŏ)

Expression. "I Miss You"
An informal way of saying "I miss you". It can be said between two people who are close to each other, such as parents and kids, or a couple. Adding "yo" at the end makes it formal (i.e., "*bogoshipoyo*").

Example)
Myung Soo: Mina, I haven't seen you for quite a long while. *Bogoshipo!*
Mina: Oppa, *bogoshipo* so much too!
Teacher: Hey guys, great to hear your voice over the phone!
Kids: Teacher, *bogoshipoyo!*

복불복 Bok Bool Bok
(bok-bul-bok)

Noun. "Take (Pot) Luck", "Crapshoot"
A compound word made up of three Chinese words: "복" *bok* ("luck") "불" *bool* ("not") "복" *bok* ("luck") = "lucky or unlucky", referring to a situation where someone has no option but to take their chances and let fate decide.

Example)
Hyori: Oh god, I wish I could know in advance which of the mystery boxes have our oppa's belongings!
Sua: You can't. It's all *bok bool bok*, you know?

볼매 Bol Mae
(bol-mae)

Noun. "The More I Look, the More Charming Someone Is"
An abbreviation for "볼수록 매력" *bol soo rok* (the more I look) *mae ryeok* (charm). It refers to someone whose charms are revealed/discovered throughout continued encounters. It can also refer to someone who might not be the love-at-first-sight type, but over time grows on someone or becomes magnetic.

Example)
Youngmi: Hey, I heard you are still seeing that guy?
Tina: Right... I told you he wasn't exactly my style, but the more I get to know him, the more attractive he is.
Youngmi: Can you elaborate? What makes him such a *bol mae*?
Tina: He accidentally dropped a wallet one time and it was full of $100 bills. Second time that happened, it had even more!
Youngmi: *B O L M A E!*

본방사수 Bon Bang Sa Soo
(bon-bang-sa-su)

Noun. "Making Sure to Watch the Original Airing of a Show"
A compound word made up of "본방" *bon bang* ("original airing") + "사수" sa soo ("defending, securing something to the death"). Hence, it is a strong resolution to watch the original airing of a TV show, instead of reruns. It is extremely important because viewership ratings are only based on 본방's and idols often request their fans to do this, so they can get a good viewership rating (= they will get more TV appearance opportunities!)

Example)
Fan Club Leader: What are we going to do to back up our oppas tonight?
Everybody: WE WILL *BON BANG SA SOO* OUR OPPA'S SHOW TONIGHT!

본좌 Bon Jwa
(bon-jwa)

Noun. "The Dominant One"
It is most widely used in online game leagues (e.g., League of Legends and Starcraft) to refer to the champion.

Example)
Junho: Move aside! Yohan coming through!
Wang: WTH? Who is he?
Junho: How dare you! This is *Bon Jwa* of StarCraft!
Wang: Oh your Majesty! I beg you to forgive my rudeness. Your gold-plated keyboard and mouse are set up here.

부비부비 Boo Bi Boo Bi
(bu-bi-bu-bi)

Phrase. <mark>"Grinding"</mark>
A type of dirty dancing where a girl stands in front of a guy, placing her hips close to his crotch and. Then she would start rubbing while he places his hands on her pelvis and holds her. It can be used to refer to any kind of sexy or suggestive dancing that involves close body contact.

Example)
Wonhee: Gross! This drunk dude was doing *boo bi boo bi* on me!
Nancy: Was he good looking?
Wonhee: No!
Nancy: Oh gross!

부킹 Booking

Noun. <mark>"Mini-Dates Set up by Night Club Waiters"</mark>
A common Korean club practice where night club waiters guide women patrons to men's tables and set up instant "mini-dates".

Example)
Waiter: Hey gentlemen, are you guys up for some *booking* tonight?
Gentlemen: Heck yeah! That's why we got a table here!

불금 Bool Geum
(bul-gŭm)

Noun. <mark>"Friday Night Fever"</mark>
An abbreviation for "불타는" *bool ta neun* ("burning") "금요일" *geum yo il* ("Friday"). It is the most cherished day by students and workers who are on a five-day work/business platform. It is an independence/liberation day for those who have been forever longing for the moment. It is called "burning" because their passion and energy is so hot.

Example)
Julio: Bro, do you know what day it is?
Brian: Uh… Friday?

Julio: Dude you are no fun. It's not just Friday, it is *bool guem*!
Brian: I have to work tonight.
Julio: Oh.

불펌 Bool Peom
(bul-p'ŏm)

Noun. "Sharing a Post Without Permission"
An abbreviation for "불법" *bool beop* ("illegal") "펌" *peom* ("sharing").
This happens when the original poster explicitly prohibits the act of sharing a post, but someone, finds a way to do just that.

Example)
Hyun: Mira, did you see their secret photo they posted in the private forum? I just uploaded to my Facebook page!
Mira: Yeah, but how… isn't that invasion of privacy or something?
Hyun: Duh, everything on the Internet is copyright free!
Mira: Oh no… you should check the forum rules to make sure it's not a *bool peom*.
Hyun: Read it and deleted it.

Bromance

Noun. "Very Close Friendship Between Two Males"
A compound word made up of "brother" and "romance". It refers to a very close friendship but platonic love between two males, often to a degree that is almost similar to that of a romantic couple.

Example)
Daesong and Songyu are literally spending their lives together! Eating, playing, and even sleeping together. There's so much *bromance* going on, but they are as straight as a ruler – they like girls so much.

버퍼링 Buffering

Noun. "Delay"
Originally it refers to a situation where a multimedia element on a web page is not loading/streaming fast enough for a pleasant viewing

experience. In Korea, however, it is also used to describe someone whose talking is unclear (e.g., stuttering, or being equivocal/evasive) so that it takes a long time to get to the point.

Example)
Tommy: Ho…ho…ho…ho…ho…l…y…
Semi: Stop *buffering* and say it already!
Tommy: Shit.

버닝 Burning

Noun. "Zealously/Passionately/Fierecely Doing Something"
The state of a mind that is deeply immersed in something. For example, "burning Friday" means that you are going to enjoy your Friday to the extreme.

Example)
Son: Yes! It's bool guem! Let's have a *burning* Friday!
Mom: What? Burning? Fire?
Son: No mom!

버로우 Burrow

Noun. "Hide", "Disappear", "Vanish"
Originated from a fictional Starcraft (computer game) species, Zerg, whose characters hide underneath the surface to attack their enemies. It is used to describe someone who suddenly disappears. This skill is used most often when someone realizes they are losing an online debate.

Example)
Kyuho: There is this one dude who keeps saying that 9.11 terrorist attack was committed by the aliens.
Joy: That can't be true…
Kyuho: Yup, after a bunch of guys posted links debunking his claim, he just *burrowed.*

버터페이스 Butter Face

Noun. "Female With Not-so-Attractive Looks"
A disparaging term in disguise. While it sounds like a compliment, it actually goes like this "She's almost perfect. She is well-educated, comes from a well-to-do family, and has a great body… Oh, *BUT HER FACE…*"

Example)
Tom: Hey man, so tell me about your girlfriend.
John: Sure, she is smart, loaded, funny… *butter face…*
Sonya: WTF? I heard you!
John: I meant that your face is so smooth, like butter!
Sonya: You are so dead.

별다방 Byeol Da Bang
(byŏl-da-bang)

Noun. "Starbucks"
"별" *byeol* means "star", and "다방" *dabang* means "coffee shop" or "tea house". This is where people buy coffee that's more expensive than their lunch!

Example)
Barry: Come meet me at *byeol da bang* at six, cool?
Tony: You mean Starbucks, right?
Barry: Welcome to 2016, man.

병맛 Byeong Mat
(byŏng-mat)

Noun. "Insane, Wacko, Crazy, and Horrible"
An abbreviation for "병신" *byeong shin* ("retard") "같은" *gat eun* ("~like") "맛" *mat* ("flavor/taste"), which literally means "tastes like a retard". While it is not clear what a retard tastes like, kids and teenagers frequently use this term to describe a situation/someone that is just weird and inexplicable.

Example)
Taekwon: Damn! Did you see how he miss the penalty kick?

THE KPOP DICTIONARY

Samson: How the heck did he miss that?

Taekwon: He's been so *byeong mat* lately... He should consider retiring.

변태 Byuntae
(byŏn-t'ae)

Noun. "Pervert"

A character which often appears in K-Dramas and Movies, they scare the female protagonists by displaying their sexual desires in an unhealthy way. Usually the male protagonist shows up and saves her (by covering her eyes with his hands).

Example)

Layla: Hey, what are you doing?

Mason: I am taking a nap in the arms of Sora.

Layla: Is that a blow-up doll with her picture printed on?

Mason: Yeah, isn't she so lovely?

Layla: You are the biggest *byuntae* I've ever seen...

콜 Call
(kol)

Phrase. "Accept"

A term derived from poker, where a player "accepts" another player's intention to raise the bet. It is widely used as an everyday term among the younger population.

Example)

Hoon: Yo, I'm going to hit the bar tonight. You want to join?

Mike: *Call*!

CARTEL

Noun. "The Union of Three Most Powerful Fan Clubs"

Reference to the alliance of the three most powerful fan clubs formed at the 2008 Dream Concert which created Black Ocean against Girls Generation. It is a form of protest where fans in the audience dress in all black and do not use any light sticks, thereby creating complete darkness. Cassiopeia +

Triple S + ELF = CARTEL.

Example)
Qiang: Did you see the black ocean created by *CARTEL* yesterday?
Tony: Yeah, it was awesome… They are like the United Nations of KPOP.

캐스팅 Casting

Noun. "Getting Hired for a Role"
Signing a contract for a role/position in a drama, a movie, a CF, or a TV show.

Example)
Seunghun got the *casting* as a leading male actor for an upcoming movie titled 'Love You So Much'.

CF

Noun. "Commercial"
An abbreviation for "commercial film". CFs are enormously influential in Korea. Many nameless entertainers can become famous overnight if a CF goes viral.

Example)
Damn, who's that girl in that Soju *CF*? She is smoking hot!
My bias, Johan's got a *CF* for a new ice cream bar! Oh dear, I am going to get so fat…

차도남/차도녀 Cha Do Nam/Nyeo
(cha-do-nam/nyŏ)

Noun. "Chic City Guy/Lady"
An abbreviation for "차가운" *cha ga un* ("cold, offish"), "도시의" *do shi e* ("urban, city"), "남자/여자" *nam ja/yeo ja* ("guy/lady"). It is a popular type of character in K-Dramas, often portrayed as a colleague or superior at work, who (generally) opens up their heart and embraces the main character and eventually falls in love.

Example)
Noah: What's up with that new girl? She's acting like there is no one above her.
Jordan: Yeah, she is one *cha do nyeo*. She's playing hard to get… She's like a New Yorker!
Tanya: New York my ass! Didn't you guys know? She's actually a hick from the country side and that's why she's acting all cold to cover that up.

재벌 Chaebol
(jae-bŏl)

Noun. "Conglomerate"

Most popular characters in K-Dramas with a Cinderella-type story line. Usually, it is a young son or sometimes a daughter of the company's chairman. They are cocky, arrogant, and believes that money can buy anything, including love. They are called chaebol 2-Se, which literally means "the second generation of the chaebol family".

Example)
The new drama featuring Koyo looks like another Cinderella story! I am pretty sure I can predict how the story will unfold… That *Chaebol 2-Se* guy will fall in love with a poor girl from the country side and she will reform him into a humble man with the power of true love.

철벽녀 Cheol Byeok Nyeo
(ch'ŏl-byŏng-nyŏ)

Noun. "Woman Who Plays Hard-to-Get"

"철" *cheol* means "iron", "벽" *byeok* means "wall", and "녀" *nyeo* means "woman". So it refers to an impregnable woman who does not open her heart easily, or accepts other people's love. In K-Drama, this is the most common type of female character. They are extremely offish at the beginning, and then slowly and gradually open their heart. But of course, they keep hiding their emotions, just to tantalize the viewers.

Example)
May: Man, I am calling it quits! I've been asking her out since high school and she keeps saying no!
Jorge: Yeah man, she is such a *cheol byeok nyeo*! Oh wait, maybe she is a

lesbian?

철새팬 Cheol Sae Fan
(ch'ŏl-sae-p'aen)

Noun. <mark>"Multifans"</mark>
"철새" *cheol sae* means "migratory bird", so when used in conjunction with "fan", it refers to someone who is a fan of multiple groups at the same time. "다팬" *da fan*, also meaning "multi-fan" can be used interchangeably.

Example)
Urias: I love Sensation Trio, but I also love Medium Bang.
Toby: Um, didn't you say that you love AAA?
Urias: I know… I am such a *cheol sae fan*.

천조국 Cheon Jo Guk
(ch'ŏn-jo-guk)

Noun. <mark>"United States of America"</mark>
Internet slang which literally means "1,000 Trillion Nation". Originated from the fact the amount of military spending by the U.S.A. is close to 1,000 trillion dollars, which is greater than the sum of many advanced nations' budgets.

Example)
Victor: I am going to *cheon jo guk* tomorrow.
Wendy: Huh? Where?
Victor: U.S.A., stupid!

정말 Cheongmal (Jeongmal)
(jŏng-mal)

Interjection. <mark>"Really"</mark>
Used to express surprise or to ask the validity of a certain situation or statement.

Example)

Hyoju: *Cheongmal cheongmal* saranghae!
Gibeom: *Cheongmal*?
Hyoju: *Cheongmal*!

첫콘/막콘 Cheot Con/Mak Con
(ch'ŏt-k'on/mak-k'on)

Noun. **"First Concert/Last Concert"**
"첫" *cheot* and "막" *mak* are an adjectives meaning "first" and "last",
respectively, so it is used when more than one concert date is available.

Example)
Henry: Angelita's cheot con is tomorrow!
Min: Nah... I will just go to their *mak con*...
Henry: Dude! *Cheot con*s are always the best!

첫사랑 Cheot Sarang
(ch'ŏt-sa-rang)

Noun. **"First Love"**
A commonly used theme for many K-Dramas, often breaking onto the
scene to complicate a "love line" (a map of relationships) of a protagonist,
who agonizes over his choice of women.

Example)
Bruce: It's been 3 years since Hyomin retired, but I just can't let her go.
Myong: I understand. *Cheot sa rang*'s are difficult to forget.

치맥 Chi Maek
(ch'i-maek)

Noun. **"Chicken and Beer"**
An abbreviation for "치킨" (chicken) and "맥주" (*maekju*, "beer"), it is
one of the favorite adult Korean snacks/meal, especially when watching a
sporting event. It usually comes plain fried or with a spicy sauce. It can be
likened to chicken wings and beer in the west. It gained massive popularity
in China thanks to the mega-hit K-Drama "My Love from the Star", where
Cheon Song-I the heroine of the drama, says "Chi Maek is perfect for a

snowy day". This line triggered the Chinese people to flock to specialty fried chicken shops. Uploading selfies with a piece of fried chicken and beer became a trend on social networks.

Example)
Joe: Oh! The soccer match is on!
Walter: Shoot! Forgot to order c*hi maek*!

친추 Chin Choo
(ch'in-ch'u)

Noun. "Adding Someone As a Friend on Social Media"
An abbreviation for "친구" *chin goo* ("friend") "추가" *choo ga* ("addition"). This is the 21st-century Facebook-era version of exchanging contact information and is considered a less aggressive and indirect way of asking for someone's contact info, such as a phone number.

Example)
Miyako: Hi, thanks for the *chin choo*!
Tomo: My pleasure!

친삭 Chin Sak
(ch'in-sak)

Noun. "Deleting Someone As a Friend on Social Media"
An abbreviation for "친구" *chin goo* ("friend") and "삭제" *sak je* ("deletion"). While it is a convenient way to end a relationship, it could be considered rude or offensive, especially when done without notice.

Example)
Miyako: Remember that Tomo kid who added me on Facebook? He seems like a stalker!
Jackie: Go ahead and *chin sak* him!

진짜 Chincha (Jinjja)
(jin-tcha)

Interjection. "Really"
Used to express surprise or to ask the validity of a certain situation/statement.

Example)
Paulina: Did you hear the news? Mimi and Changyo are dating!
Kathryn: *Chincha*?

친구 Chingu
(ch'in-'gu)

Noun. "Friend", "Buddy"
Although two people can be friends regardless of their age, chingu is exclusively used for a person of the same age/grade in school. Others are addressed as "선배" *sunbae* ("senior") and "후배" *hoobae* ("junior")
Example)
Since they both come from the 96-line, they became *chingu*.

초보 Chobo
(ch'o-bo)

Noun. "Newbie"
A compound word made up of two Chinese words: "초" *cho* ("first") "보" *bo* ("step"), which became a popular term among online gamers around the world, thanks to ubiquitous Korean gamers who contributed to the burgeoning of world's largest e-sports (Starcraft, LOL, Counter Strike, and etc.) league.

Example)
Nick: I just started playing Star Craft yesterday.
Tim: Dude, you must be such a *chobo*.

Chocolate Abs

Noun. "Six Pack"
So called because chiseled abs look similar to blocks of chocolate.

Example)
Dongjoon's been working out so hard for the past 6 months. Look at his *chocolate abs!* Oh, I bet I can use that as a washboard.

초딩 Choding
(ch'o-ding)

Noun. "Someone Who Acts Like a Kid"
An elementary school student. This term is also used to make fun of someone who acts like a kid.

Example)
Jihoon's favorite dishes are pizza, hamburger, and French fries. He has such a *choding* appetite.
Kay just passed out after playing a video game for 10 hours non-stop. He is still a *choding* at heart!

출첵 Chool Chek
(ch'ul-ch'ek)

Noun. "Roll Call"
An abbreviation for "출석" *chool seok* ("attendance") + check". It is the first activity at the beginning of a school day in Korea. Some teachers opt for a visual check, some kids take advantage of this, by removing and hiding their desks and chairs to fool the teachers into thinking there is no one absent.

Example)
Student A: (Typing a text message) Dude, hurry the hell up! Teacher's about to do a *chool check!*
Student B: What! I overslept! On my way!

(20 munutes later)

Student B: Hey… It says we don't have school today?
Student A: I Can't believe you fell for that! It's a national holiday today. LOL.
Student B: A nwa…

춤 Choom
(ch'um)

Noun. "Dance"
Considered to be one of the essential virtues/skills an idol should possess.

Example)
Tiny Baby's signature move is the propeller *choom*. She does look like a little helicopter about to take off!

추석 Chuseok
(ch'u-sŏk)

Noun. "Tradtional Korean Holiday in the Autum"
A major harvest festival in Korea which lasts for three days. It is celebrated on the 15th day of the 8th month of the lunar calendar. It is also called "Hangawi" which comes from archaic Korean. People often dress up in hanbok and engage in traditional activities.

Example)
Michelle is wearing Hanbok to celebrate *Chuseok* with her family.

취중진담 Chwi Joong Jin Dam
(ch'wi-jung-jin-dam)

Noun. "Drunk Confession", "In Wine There is Truth"
A compound word made up of "취중" *chwi joong* ("while drunk") + "진담" *jin dam* ("telling the truth"). It is the act of admitting one's true feelings toward somebody, with the help of alcohol because they find it difficult to do so when sober. While many use it as an opportunity to ask someone out, others use it to raise hell with someone. It is a very useful tactic because if it doesn't go the way you expected, you can always put the

blame on alcohol (e.g., "Wow, I don't remember saying that!"). It is also the name of a popular song by Kim Dong-ryul.

Example)
Mimi: I can't believe he asked me out last night. I guess he was too drunk and just being goofy.
Yolanda: Hm, you never know, maybe he was making a *chwi joong jin dam*.

취켓팅 Chwicketing
(ch'wi-k'et-t'ing)

Noun. "Ticketing for Cancelled Tickets"
If you happen to lose out during the initial bloodbath of ticketing, there's always a second chance through "취켓팅", or "canceled ticketing". "취" *chwi* comes from the word "취소" *chwi so*, which means "cancellation," which Korean fans have combined with the word "ticketing." Fans use this term to refer to ticketing for canceled tickets. Often fans will stay up until 4 AM in order to catch canceled tickets on ticketing websites.

Example)
Inbi: Ugh! All tickets are sold out!
Bonnie: Don't give up just yet! There is always a chance for *chwicketing*!

콜라보 Colabo

Noun. "Collaboration"
The practice through which artists join forces to create a unique piece of work that incorporates the distinctive characters of each contributing artist.

Example)
Penny: Wow! Hyunie Honey and Timber are making a *colabo* album!
Mark: Can't wait to see that!

컴백 Comeback

Noun. "Returning of an Idol After Hiatus"
The return of an idol singer or a group, which entails a new single/album release. It is often followed by appearing on TV music shows to showcase their new work.

Example)
Did you hear? JooJoo is making a *comeback* with their new digital single! She will be on Inkigayo this Saturday!

Concept

Noun. "Image or Character One Chooses to Pursue"
An image or a character which an idol singer or a group assumes. It can be either career-long or as short as for a single TV show. It can change frequently, depending on the overall theme of their goal. For example, one can have "sexy" as their theme for their new album, but can choose to have "comical" as their theme for the next album.
Example)
Wow, Hyunhwa really came back with a sexy *concept* she promised... She no longer embraces that cute girl *concept* which wasn't so successful.

D Line

Noun. "Body with Protruding Belly"
A term describing the shape of a body where the belly is protruding either due to pregnancy or drinking too much beer, thereby resembling the letter "D". Unlike "S Line", this is the type of body idols don't want.

Example)
Look at Mingyo's beer belly! He used to have chocolate abs but now he is a total *D Line* itself.

다음 Da Eum
(da-ŭm)

Noun. "Next", "Later"
Also the name of Korea's second-largest Internet portal.

Example)
Hoon: Hey Sohee, I've got a whole collection of WAWA's pictures you
might like. Do you like this? This? What about this?
Sohee: Hm… *Da Eum! Da Eum!* Oh, stop I like this one.

다나까 Da Na Ka
(da-na-kka)

Phrase. "Military Style Talking"
Military-style talking where every sentence has to end in either Da, Na, or
Ka, which are the formal/official tones of the Korean language. It became
extremely popular thanks to the mega-hit K-Drama Descendants of the Sun,
a romantic story with a military battlefield as the backdrop.

Example)
Girl: Doc, my boyfriend has been acting weird lately.
Doc: What's the matter?
Girl: His sentences all end in *~da, ~na, ~ka.*
Doc: Oh, is he in the army?
Girl: Impossible. He was too obese to go to the army.

답정너 Dab Jeong Neo
(dap-chŏng-nŏ)

Noun. "Askhole"
Someone who constantly asks for your advice but always does whatever
they want. (Why ask then?).

Example)
Girlfriend: Honey, should I wear the pink dress or the blue dress?
Boyfriend: I think the blue one looks good on you.

Girlfriend: Hm, I will just wear the pink one.
Boyfriend: You are a *dab jeong neo*, aren't you?

대륙 Dae Ryuk
(dae-ryuk)

Noun. `"China"`

Literal meaning is "continent" or "land mass". The term, mostly used among the younger generation on the Internet, became a nickname for China, due to the fact that the country boasts a massive amount of land and population. It is most frequently used in the form of "대륙의" *dae ryuk eui* ~sth = "sth of China". For example, "대륙의 기상 (*gi sang*"spirit")" is "The Spirit of China".

Example)
Xiao: Look at me! I just ate 30 dumplings for lunch!
Tomo: Man, that's what I call *dae ryuk* style!

대박 Daebak
(dae-bak)

Noun. `"Jackpot", "Incredible"`

A term that can be used to express amazement and excitement. Can be translated as "jackpot", "big win" "awesome" or "incredible".

Example)
KOKO's new digital single all-killed the charts! It sure is a *daebak* album!
I just saw Alisha in Myeongdong! *D-A-E-B-A-K!*

대상 Daesang
(dae-sang)

Noun. `"Grand Prize", "Top Award"`

Most prestigious award one can receive.

Example)
Wow! Soye won the *daesang* at KBC's Diamond Disk Awards!

닥살 Dak Sal
(dak-sal)

Noun. <mark>"Goosebumps" "Disgusting"</mark>
In Korean, it has a dual meaning – 1) Disgusting (negative) - when seeing a couple performing a PDA (public display of affection) 2) Goose bumps (positive) - when watching your favorite bias perform on the stage.

Example)
(At a KPOP idol concert)

Fan Girl 1: OMG!!!!!!!!!!! OMG!!!!!!!!
Fan Girl 2: OPPA! I LOVE YOU!!!!!!!
Fan Girl 3: MARRY ME!!!!!!!!!!!!!!!!!
Fan Girl 1: LOL I feel like a chicken. Look at all these *dak sal*.
Fan Girl 2 & 3: Buc Buc Buc Buc? Buc Buc Buc Buc!

단톡 Dan Tok
(dan-tok)

Noun. <mark>"Group Chat"</mark>
One of the many functions provided by Kakao Talk, a popular chat app, where one can invite other users to talk in a group setting. While the intentions are good, in most cases, many employees feel like falling into a hell hole when it is created by their workplace boss, who uses it to monitor and control subordinates.

Example)
Sumi: Hey, can you please invite me to the *dan tok* room?
Lola: Are you sure? Our boss will send texts non-stop!

당근 Dang Geun
(dang-gŭn)

Phrase. <mark>"Fo' Sho"</mark>
Literally means "carrot", but it is also a mutated/fun version of the phrase " 당연" *dang yeon* ("of course/absolutely").

Example)
Mom: Did you have carrots today?
Son: *Dang geun!*
Mom: Yes, carrots.
Son: Oh I mean, of course!

다크호스 Dark Horse

Noun. "A Little Known Candidate or Competitor Who Emerges to Prominence"
A 19th-century horse racing slang which is more popularly used in Korea than other English speaking countries. You can hear the word in "variety" TV shows that involve competition, such as Our Neighborhood Arts and Physical Education (Cool Kiz On The Block).

Example)
Michael: Ha! You didn't know I've been practicing Star Craft every day for the tournament, did you?
Sam: Damn, man! You da real *dark horse* now!

대시 Dash

Noun. "To Make a Move"
"Asking someone out", and is also used in the verb form "대시하다" *dash hada*. Valentine's Day and Christmas Day are among the most popular days for this.

Example)
Minho: I really like her, but I am not sure if she will say yes if I asked her out…
Samantha: Duh, there is only one way to find out! *Dash*!

DB

Chat Acronym. "Cig"
An acronym made up by taking the initial consonants of the word "담배" *dam bae* ("cigarette"). It is mostly used by teenagers who are under the legal age for smoking, to avoid detection by adults (e.g., parents, teachers,

and etc.)

Example)
Sam: Hurry! Quick! Gimme yo *DB*!
Juno: Ain't got none. I quit it cold turkey, brah!

DBSK

Noun. "Dong Bang Shin Ki"
Korean abbreviation of Dong Bang Shin Ki, which is the second most
commonly used acronym after the Chinese version TVXQ.

Example)
Chin: Do you know what *DBSK* means?
Ursula: Yes. Dong Bang Shin Ki!

따봉 Dda Bong
(tda-bong)

Phrase. "Thumbs Up"
An expression used to display amazement or satisfaction, with your
thumb(s) up. It is actually a Portuguese word "Está bom", which means
"It is good". It became extremely popular thanks to an orange juice TV
commercial in the 1980s, which shows a group of Korean buyers visiting
an orange farm in Brazil. Upon inspection, he says the word with his thumb
up, and the farmers go crazy in excitement, all dancing the Samba. Ever
since then, it has been synonymous with "The Best".

Example)
Mom: Son, what do you say I raise your allowance?
Son: *Dda bong*!

딸바보 Ddal Babo
(tdal-ba-bo)

Noun. "Daughter's Daddy"
Literal meaning is "daughter-stupid", which can be roughly translated as
"daughter-crazy". It refers to a daddy who adores, is crazy about, and

willing to do anything for his daughter. This is to the point that it makes him love-blind, thereby looking like a babo (fool). The term became popular because of a popular reality TV show "The Return of Superman" which featured awe-provoking episodes of Choo Seong-hoon and his adorable daughter Sarang-i.

Example)
Tina: Damn, John is with her daughter 24/7.
Thomas: Yeah, he is such a *ddal babo*.

뜬금포 Ddeun Geum Po
(tdŭn-'gŭm-p'o)

Noun. "Something Ttotally Unexpected/Random"
"뜬금" ddeun geum means "random" or "unexpected" and 포 (po) means "firing (a weapon)". It originally means an unexpected home run in baseball, but has recently made its way into everyday conversation. If someone says something out of the blue, you say this.

Example)
Kyle: Um, I think I want to thank you for being my friend.
Donnie: Huh? Why? That was a *ddeun geum po*.

또라이 Ddo Ra I
(tdo-ra-i)

Noun. "Freak"
Originally used to refer to someone with mental illness, but it is used to describe someone who is wild and daring, going beyond the limits of common sense or basic values.

Example)
Mendy: Look at me! I ate a whole tube of wasabi! Bwahahaha!
Justin: You are just a *ddo ra i*, man…

똥차 Ddong Cha
(tdong-ch'a)

Noun. "Ex-boyfriend"

A compound word made up of "똥" *ddong* ("poop") + "차" *cha* ("car"),
meaning "honey wagon". The word 똥 is used as a prefix to emphasize that
something is of low quality. It is a figurative expression referring to an ex-
boyfriend who had disappointed and hurt you, and is often used as "forget
the ddong cha and wait for a brand new Mercedes (new relationship)."

Example)
Fei: Ha! That *ddong cha* keeps calling me! I wonder what he's up to now?
Judy: Huh? Are you trying to buy a used car?
Fei: No, I meant my ex-boyfriend.

득템 Deuk Tem
(dŭk-t'em)

Noun. "Getting a Good Deal on Something"

A term that originated from MMORPG (Massively Multiplayer Online
Role-playing Games), where a player gains the abandoned item of another
character, or receives something unexpected as a reward for a battle won.

Example)
Toby: Oh yes! *Dek Tem!*
John: What did you get?
Toby: I bought an iPhone 6S for $35!
John: Let me see? Hm, it says iPhome, not iPhone.
Toby: Hot dang it… Thought it was too good to be true…

듣보잡 Deut Bo Jab
(dŭt-po-jap)

Noun. "Someone of No Importance"

An abbreviation for "듣도" *deut do* ("ever heard") + "보도" *bo do*
("ever seen") + "못한" *mot han* ("never") + "잡 것" *jab geot* ("ragtag") =
"someone you have never heard or seen". It is used to hurt someone's self-

esteem and is most effective when used in the most condescending way possible.

Example)
Heena: Hm… Baby Dolls won a Super Star Awards. Is this big?
Uma: Nah, never heard of it. It must be a *deut bo jab.*

Digital Single

Noun. "Music Track Only Available Through Online Channels"
Music track only available through online channels (i.e., download and streaming).

Example)
It's official! Tin Tin just released their *digital single*! Available for download at Soribada now.

디스패치 Dispatch

Noun. "The CIA of the Korean Showbiz Industry"
Established in 2010, it is an Internet-based news agency that focuses on celebrity gossip and breaking news. It is currently the single most dominant agency in the industry. It is believed that many of the reporters are former entertainment reporters from SportsSeoul.com. It is most famous for delivering exclusive stories on celebrity dating scenes by what many consider as paparazzi-style yellow journalism, but fans love it.

Example)
Tony: Dang! Jaeho's on *Dispatch*!
Micky: Huh? Dispatch? It better be something good! Otherwise they are done.

도촬 Do Chwal
(to-ch'wal)

Noun. "Taking Pictures Without Permission"
It is an abbreviation for 도둑 *do dook* ("thieif") + 촬영 *chwal* yeong ("filming"). A behavior associated with someone who is a peeping tom, and

gains sexual gratification through secretly watching people undressing or engaging in sexual activities. Many KPOP idols are victimized by extreme sasaeng fans who engage in extreme measures to capture their private lives.

Example)
Mina: Hey mister! Did you just *do chwal* me?
Man: Um, I was just sending a text message with my phone. Here, mine doesn't even have a camera.
Mina: But you would have if you had a camera, right?
Man: A nwa…

Dol

Noun. "Idol"
An abbreviation for "idol", but can be attached to the end of a word to create a compound word (e.g., "beast-dol", "model-dol", "muscle-dol", or "acting-dol").
Example)
Taekyo has such an awesome body. He is my favorite *muscle-dol*.
Hyomin sure can act! She's done an awesome job as a supporting actor in the movie. She probably is the best *acting-dol* available today.

돌직구 Dol Jik Goo
(dol-jik-hu)

Noun. "Very Straight Forward Comment (Question)"
"돌" *dol* means "rock" and "직구" *jik goo* means "fast ball". Literal meaning is "a powerful (rock-solid) fastball", but is used to describe a "very straight forward comment (question)". It is most effective if used when the listener is least expecting it.

Example)
Baby: Grandma, why is mom so ugly?
Mother-in-Law: I guess babies really can't lie.
Dad: That is the most destructive *dol jik goo* I've ever heard…
Mom: …...

돌싱 Dol Sing
(dol-shing)

Noun. "Recently Divorced Person"
An abbreviation for "돌아온" *dol ah on* ("returned") "싱글" single, to mean "returned to being single" It is also used for idols who come back as a solo artist after a period of being part of a group.

Example)
Julian: Wow, who's that lady?

Yona: Oh, that's Miriam from Mexico.
Julian: Does she have a boyfriend?
Yona: All I know is that she is a *dol sing*.
Juna: Doesn't matter she was once married or not! <3 <3

동안 Dong An
(dong-an)

Noun. "Face That Looks Younger Than Actual Age"
A face that looks younger than actual age. This is a huge compliment, especially for a female idol.

Example)
Wonjun is in his 30's but he looks like a teenager. Such a *dong an* he has!

동생 Dong Saeng
(dong-saeng)

Noun. "Younger Sibling"
A term for a younger sibling, but it can be used for anyone younger, regardless of gender. It can be used in place of someone's name.

Example)
Hyoju is my favorite *dong saeng*.

Although Bohye is my *dong saeng*, she is so mature that I often feel like I am her *dong saeng*.

드라마퀸 Drama Queen

Noun. "Someone Who Responds to Situations in the Most Dramatic Way Possible"
It refers to that one friend we all have who constantly turns something trivial into a major deal, whenever the chance is given. In K-Drama settings, it is often the female protagonist's best friend, fussing over nothing and making things more complicated than necessary.

Example)
Nina: Bianca! I heard he didn't buy you a dessert! How can you let him do that? It's insane! You shouldn't let him treat you like that!
Bianca: Um… It's perfectly fine with me…?
Nina: No way! You break up with hi right now!
Bianca: Don't be a *drama queen*, please…?

Dream Concert

Noun. "Biggest Annual KPOP Concert"
The biggest annual KPOP concert where as many as 32 high-profile singer/groups participate. Each yearly renewal has a theme such as "Viva Korea" or "Cheer up Korea".

Example)
Are you going to this year's *Dream Concert*? I heard that all top 10 idol groups will perform!

드립 Drib
(dŭ-rip)

Noun. "Joke Attempt"
A term derived from the broadcast lingo "ad lib", which is saying something spontaneously, or improvising, most frequently used in sitcoms and variety shows. It often catches other co-actors off guard and causes a

series of laughter, leading to an NG.

Example)
Yena: Oh no! Jennie's got so wasted.
Robert: So wasted that she belongs in a trash can!
Yena: Oh man, that was a horrible *drib*.
Robert: Yeah I agree.

덕후 Dukhoo
(dŏ-k'u)

Noun. "Someone Who is Overly Obsessed With Something (Culture/Object)"

Originated from the Japanese term "otaku", which is often translated as "geek" or "mania", but in Korea it is thought to be more severe in its level of obsession, to the point where it becomes an object of mockery.

Example)
Kong: What are you doing, buddy?
Neal: I'm having a romantic time with my girlfriend Yumi. Can't you see?
Kong: Dude… That is just a cardboard cut out of her…
Yumi: How dare you! She is my true love!
Kong: You are such a *deok hoo*…

뒷북 Dwit Book
(dwit-puk)

Noun. "Monday Morning Quarterback (US term)", "Fuss Around After The Event", or "One Step Behind"

Someone who makes a late response and is slow in understanding.
Example)
Kiho: Hey! Do you know Gangnam Style? I heard it is the hottest KPOP now?
Youngsoo: That's a *dwit book*… That was in 2012 and we are in 2016. Get with the program, man!

에바 E Ba
(e-ba)

Phrase.

Kids' and teenagers' way of saying "over reaction", but there is a theory claiming that it is actually a compound word made up of "error + over = eva = e ba". Regardless of its origin, it is used to describe the act of going too far or exaggerating too much.

Example)
Reina: Oh my god! I think BTB oppa like me!
Joey: Why do you say that?
Reina: I got his autograph today and he drew a little heart! I think that's a secret message he's sending to me!
Joey: That's a little *e ba*… He always does that to his fans.

엑박 Ek Bak
(ek-pak)

Noun. "Image Not Found"

An abbreviation for "엑스" ("x") + "박스" box = "X-Box". It is not the name of the video game console by Microsoft, it refers to an error message caused by a broken image in a web browser, due to the file being not present or other possible issues. The error message is graphically represented by an empty box with and "x" symbol inside, hence the term.

Example)
Woody: What? Why am I getting all these *ek bak*'s? I want to see AOB's new photos!
Ming: Sorry man, our Internet has been disconnected. We haven't paid the bill for the past 6 months.

어부바 Eo Boo Ba
(ŏ-bu-ba)

Noun. "Piggy Back"

One carrying another on their back. In K-Dramas, it is often a hot guy carrying a drunk girl on his back, while the girl often expresses her affection unconsciously (i.e., too drunk).

Example)
Eunice drank so much Soju last night I had to give her a *eo boo ba*, and guess what? She unconsciously confessed that she likes me!

어장관리 Eo Jang Gwan Ri
(ŏ-jang-gwal-li)

Phrase. "Playing the Field"
Literally means "management of fishing ground", and is used to describe the act of pretending to be interested in the opposite sex, without a genuine intention to advance the relationship. The "fish" gets confused to the point where they wonder if they are in a relationship or not, but in reality they are not.

Example)
Shina: Hm, Jimmy keeps texting me every day but never asks me out. I wonder if he really likes me Wondo: Sounds fishy to me... My bet is that he is just doing *Eo Jang Gwan Ri* on you. Stay away from him!

얼빵 Eol Bbang
(ŏl-ppang)

Noun. "Ugly Face"
Opposite of "얼짱" *eol zzang* ("good looking face"). The word "얼" *eol* refers to "얼굴" *eol gool* ("face"), and "빵" *bbang* means either "zero" or "bust". Hence it could be rephrased as "Looks = score 0 or complete bust".

Example)
Boyfriend: Baby, when I'm with you, I feel like I'm dating two girls at the same time.
Girlfriend: Awww really? How? Is that a good thing?
Boyfriend: Yeah, 2 girls. One is *eol zzang* and the other is *eol bbang*. With make up on you are pretty, but without it you are ...
Girlfriend: How do you want to die?

어머니 Eomeoni (Omoni)
(ŏ-mŏ-ni)

Noun. "Mother"
Formal way of saying "엄마" *eomma* ("mom"), but can also be used to address husband's mother (mother-in-law).

Example)
Jenny: I am so nervous because *eomeoni* will be here for the weekend.
Soya: Your mother?
Jenny: No, my mother-in-law!

언플 Eon Peul
(ŏn-p'ŭl)

Noun. "Promoting Through the Media"
A Korean term that can be translated as "playing around with the media" to gain (unfair) advantage. It is termed so because entertainment companies use the media to promote their singers/groups. Common tactics include writing/disseminating press releases, news articles, and gossip creation.

Example)
Man, just today I read 5 articles about Miryo! Her company does so much *Eon Peul*!

어서 오세요 Eoseo Oseyo
(ŏ-sŏ o-se-yo)

Phrase. "Welcome" "Please Come in"
"어서" *eoseo* means "quickly", "promptly" and "오세요" *oseyo* means "please come". It is what a host says to greet guests.

Example)
(At Hong Kong International Airport)
Mingyu: Damn! Look at all these people! They think I am a KPOP Idol! Everyone is holding a sign that says *eoso oseyo*! I feel super welcomed!
Hyeon: Um... maybe not? Our schedule just coincided with a real KPOP

group.

의리 Eui Ri
(ŭi-ri)

Noun. "Loyalty"
A term that became extremely popular in 2015 after a shikye (a traditional sweet Korean rice beverage) CF featuring Kim Bo-seong, a middle-aged action movie star famous for saying the word "eui ri" repeatedly every time he has a chance (he believes "eui ri" is the most important and the manliest thing in the world. He uses it as an excuse/answer for everything he does). The CF comically incorporated the word into product descriptions (e.g., saying "Americano" as "Ame "eu ri" cano"), and became a hit. Aside from its actual meaning, people utter it simply for fun.

Example)
Bo: Yes! I finished my home work! *Eui ri*!
James: Good job, buddy! Want to go grab a beer or something?
Bo: *Eui ri*! Let's go! *Eui ri*!
James: Oh well, you don't have to say that in every sentence, but whatever makes you sleep at night...

음악 Eum Ak
(ŭ-mak)

Noun. "Music"
A compound word made up of two Chinese words - "음" *eum* means "sound" and "악" *ak* can mean "to enjoy" or "song".

Example)
What kind of *eum ak* do you like listening to the most?

응원 Eung Won
(ŭng-wŏn)

Noun. "Supporting"
In KPOP, it refers to the "fan chants" during a song which show support for

their idols, often accompanied by thunder sticks (bam bam's) or glow sticks to create a wave of "fan light".

Example)
May: Light sticks? Check! Slogans? Check!
April: It's *eung won* time!

Eye Smile

Noun. "The Shape of Eyes Becoming a Crescent While Smiling"
The shape of eyes becoming a crescent shape while smiling, thereby forming its own smile. This could be a stealthy way of flirting and showing affection.

Example)
Nina's *eye smiles* are so seductive and flirty that so many guys get fooled into thinking that she likes them.

Fan Boy/Fan Girl

Noun. "Very Passionate Fan"
A very passionate fan who is obsessed with everything their favorite idol does.

Example)
Jihye: I have bought everything related to 5 Minute – including pillow cases with their pictures printed on, vintage cassette tapes, and their discarded chewing gum!
Paul: You are such a *fan girl*, aren't you?

팬캠 Fan Cam

Noun. "Footage Taken Directly by Fans"
In contrast to those taken by professionals (e.g., photographers (paparazzi), journalists, reporters), this refers to moments (photos and videos) captured directly by fans. At concerts and fan events, you can see that everyone is holding up their smartphones. Do not confuse this with the term "sasaeng", which refers to fans going to extremes (i.e., sneaking into bias's home,

which is a criminal offense).

Example)
Jin: Dang… Juno Juno has been charged with assault!
Bernard: Yeah, I heard everything was caught on that *fan cam* after the concert.

Fan Chant

Noun. "Fans Chanting During a Performance to Show Support"
Words that are chanted by the fans in the audience during a performance or a particular song to express their support and love. It is mostly the names of the singers and is usually shouted during the part where the singers are not singing.

Example)
Lee-Joo-Bin! Lee-Joo-Bin! One and Only Lee-Joo-Bin! The members of Lee Joo Bin's fan club, One and Only, shouted their signature *fan chant*.

Fan Club

Noun. "Faction"
An organized group of fans who engage in various activities to support their idol singers or groups. They usually have their own club name, meaning, color, and often have rival fan clubs.

Example)
I really like Eun Sung so I joined the *fan club* Shooting Star! The name comes from her name Sung which means star, and the official color is bright silver just like a star in the universe.

Fan Fiction

Noun. "Fictional Tales Written by Fans Starring Their Favorite Idols"
Fictional tales written by fans starring their favorite idols. The story line usually involves conflicts and romance.

Example)
Kayla is so talented in writing *fan fictions.* I asked her to write one with me and Junho in it. Of course, I was the love of his life in the story

Fan Service

Noun. "Something Idols Do to Please Their Fans"
Something idols do to please their fans, both voluntarily and by request, such as singing a special song or making a cute gesture.

Example)
Seho Oppa! Please do the bbuing bbuing dance?
Seho puts his fists up under his eyes and moves them in circular directions saying bbuing bbuing.
Awwwww, Seho Oppa's *fan service* is the best!

Fan Wars

Noun. "Brutal Warfare Between Fan Clubs"
A brutal warfare between the fans of one idol group against the fans of another.

Example)
They totally ruined our Oppa's performance by creating a black ocean!
Argggh! It's a *fan war*!

Fandom

Noun. "Community of Fans"
A community of fans who share a common interest, empathy, and camaraderie toward idols, groups, TV shows, movies, books and etc.

Example)
I think the TV show 'I Love You, You Love Me' has the biggest *fandom* among many reality shows because they have members from 5 different idol groups.

Fashionista

Noun. "Someone Who Has a Great Sense of Fashion"
Someone who has a great sense of fashion, such as GD of Big Bang. The opposite is "Fashion Terroirst".

Example)
My Oppa can make a really good model. Not only is he tall and slim, he understands fashion. He is such a *fashionista!*

Feels

Noun. "Overwhelming Wave of Emotions"
Overwhelming wave of emotions sometimes resulting in screaming and crying, which can't be easily explained or described with words. This frequently occurs while watching K-Dramas or KPOP MV's.
Example)
The lyrics of J-Pay's new song is so romantic that watching J-Pay's MV gives me the *feels*, fooling my mind to think I am in love with him.

화이팅 Fighting/Hwaiting
(hwa-i-t'ing)

Phrase. "Cheers. Let's fight!. Let's Go!"
Something that is said to promote a sense of unity. It can be said to show support for someone, especially in sports events. In a monologue, it is used to give the speaker a confidence boost.

Example)
Korea vs. Japan soccer game tonight! Team Korea *fighting!*
Okay, I can do this… *fighting!*
Hey sis, heard you are having an exam today. *Fighting!*

Flower Boy

Noun. "Incredibly Good Looking Young Male"
An incredibly attractive young male whose beauty (mostly looks) is

comparable to that of a flower.

Example)
How can a man be so beautiful? Taeyong is such a *flower boy*.

가지마 Ga Ji Ma
(ga-ji-ma)

Phrase. `"Don't Go"`
A magical word that is used at the most dramatic moment of a K-Drama or KPOP M/V. It has an enchanting power that glues together a couple on the verge of breaking up. It is most often used after an intense argument, and just when one decides to leave, the other summons up all their courage and says this, often followed by a back hug.

Example)
Girlfriend: We are over. Good bye. It's been fun.
Boyfriend: *Ga ji ma!*
Girnfriend: Why?
Boyfriend: Can you spare me $5? I have no taxi money.

갑/을 Gab/Eul
(gab/ŭl)

Noun. `"Upper-Hand/Lower Hand"`
A term used to describe the power dynamic between two people, usually in contractual settings. Gab is the one with the upper-hand while Eul is the subjugated party.

Example)
YOYO Entertainment is the *gab* while Honggi is the *eur*, bound by a contract. Honggi pretty much has to do whatever YOYO Entertainment orders him to do.

개취 Gae Chwi
(gae-ch'wi)

Phrase. "Personal Preference"
An abbreviation for "개인" *gae in* ("individual/personal") "취향" *chwi hyang* ("preference"). Although it has the term gae, it is not the gae used to emphasize (as in "개이득" *gae i deuk*, it is just an abbreviation for gae in. This word is strongly associated with the term Otaku, someone who is overly obsessed with something (culture/subject), to the point of being a target of mockery.

Example)
Jenny: This is my detox juice! Coconut water, Tabasco, Kimchi soup, and olive oil.
Mark: Ewwwwwwwwwwwwww.
Jenny: Excuse me, can you please respect people's *gae chwi?*

개이득 Gae Ideuk
(gae-i-dŭk)

Phrase. "Awesome Gain" or "Huge Profit"
The term gae literally means dog, which has many meanings aside from its original meaning when it is used in combination with other words, it emphasizes the word, just like the F word in English. Ideuk (not Iteuk from Super Junior) means "profit" or "gain".

Example)
Felix: I bought this laptop for $300 and sold it on eBay for $500!
Jose: Wow! That's some nice gain you made right there.
Felix: Not just a normal gain, it is *gae ideuk.*

무개념 Gae Nyeom
(mu-gae-nyŏm)

Noun. "Shameless"
무 *moo* ("nothing", "non-existent" + "개념" *gae nyeom* ("concept", "idea"), referring to someone who is clueless about what's going on around

THE KPOP DICTIONARY

him/her, similar to 진상 *jin sang*.

Example)
Laughing out loud at someone's funeral is a prime example of *moo gae nyeom*.

갠소 Gaen So
(gaen-so)

Noun. "Private Collection"
A teen's way of abbreviating the word "개인" *gae in* ("personal") + 소장 *so jang* ("collection"). It refers to the downloading and storing of a rare picture of your favorite bias, with no intention of sharing it with others.

Example)
(Tony sees a sexy picture of his bias on the Internet)
Tony: *Gaen so…* Straight to my private collection…

갈비 Galbi
(gal-bi)

Phrase. "Becoming More and More Unlikable"
An abbreviation for "갈수록" *gal soo rok* ("becoming more ~sth") + "비호감" *bi ho gam* ("Mr./Ms. Unlikable"). It refers to someone who really gets on your nerves, and gets worse every day, showing no sign of improvement. Someone who you want to avoid at all costs.

Example)
Rosario: Ugh! Guess what he did today? He farted in my face.
Mina: Last time he made you eat his booger and he farts in your face? Getting worse every time, girl… He is such a *gal bi*.

감 Gam
(gam)

Noun. "Hunch"
An indescribable (but surprisingly accurate) gut feeling you get in a

decisive situation. It could be the result of remembering a similar experience you had in the past or some other mysterious reason (e.g., divine intervention?).

Example)
Hoon: I have a *gam* that she is not a wife material. My *gam* is always right.
Joey: Sure. Your 3 ex-wives will agree with that.

감독 Gamdok
(gam-dok)

Noun. "Coach (in Sports)", "(Movie) Director"
It refers to the person who oversees the production of a program or the management of a sports team.

Example)
The movie K-Pop Legends was Baemin's debut work as a movie *gamdok*.

강추 Gang Choo
(gang-ch'u)

Phrase. "Strongly Recommended"
An abbreviation for "강력추천" *gang ryeok choo cheon*. The word "강력" *gang ryeok* and "추천" *choo cheon* are Chinese words which mean "strong/ powerful" and "recommendation", respectively. If a fangirl/fanboy's bias uses this on a product, it works as a strong endorsement which magically opens up their wallet.

Example)
Murielle: Did you see? How was our oppa's new M/V?
Helen: One word. *Gang Choo!*
Murielle: It must be another big hit!

강남 Gangnam
(gang-nam)

Noun. "Wealthy District in Seoul"

A wealthy district in Seoul. The literal meaning is "South of the River", and it is termed so that it refers to the south of the "Han River" that runs through the middle of Seoul.

Example)
You want to go to Hongdae and get drunk on the cheap? Or, we can chill in *Gangnam* with style!

강남스타일 Gangnam Style

Noun. "Ultra Mega Hit Song by Psy"
An ultra super mega hit song by Psy which became a world-wide phenomenon with its signature "horse riding dance".

Example)
Op, op, Oppa *Gannam Style!*.
Gangnam Style introduced K-Pop to so many who had no idea where Korea was even located.

간지 Ganji
(gan-ji)

Noun. Adjective. "Fashionable", "Stylish", "Cool", "Swag"
Originated from the Japanese word kanji ("feeling" and "impression"), it is used to express admiration or awe.

Example)
Tim: New Nike shoes, new Gucci hat, new Prada shades… In total, my *ganji* score increased by +50.
Bo: And your bankroll decreased by -100,000,000.

가온차트 Gaon Chart

Noun. "The Only Official Music Ranking Chart"
The only official music ranking chart certified by the KOCCA (Korea Creative Content Agency). It provides relatively trustworthy standards as it discounts mass purchases (downloads) when rating songs for chart position, a common entertainment company practice in an attempt to manipulate chart rankings.

Example)
Color Pop just topped the *Gaon Chart!* This is big!

가사 Gasa
(ga-sa)

Noun. "Lyrics"
One of the many essential elements that make up a good piece of music.
Idols who can sing the lyrics with their hearts are extremely talented and
rare.

Example)
Angel Mio, a singer-song-writer composed the music and wrote the *gasa*
for the song.

가슴 Gaseum
(ga-sŭm)

Noun. "The Chest (body)", "Heart"
A vital organ of your body. Metaphorically, where the emotions come from
and are felt.

Example)
Ever since my bias group Nero Nero broke up, my *gaseum* hurts every now
and then.

가싶남 Gaship Nam
(ga-shim-nam)

Noun. "Man Who I Want to Possess"
An abbreviation for "가지고 싶은 남자" *gajigo* ("to possess") *shipeun*
("want to~") *namja* ("man"). It can be used to describe a fan girl's fantasy,
or as a compliment paid to someone who is attractive. But when used by a
stan or sa saeng fan, things can get serious. This term frequently appears in
fan fiction stories.

Example)

Ursula: What do you want for Christmas?
Miho: Jaemin oppa! I really want to possess him!
Ursula: So he's your *gasip nam*!

가요 Gayo
(ga-yo)

Noun. "Korean Pop Music"
Originally used to refer to the whole category of "popular music", but with
the advent of KPOP, it became synonymous with "Korean Pop Music" over
the globe.

Example)
My favorite *gayo* is Diamond 5's Eternal Love.

가요대전 Gayo Daejeon
(ga-yo-dae-jŏn)

Noun. "Annual End-of-the-Year KPOP Music Festvial"
An annual end-of-the-year KPOP music festival hosted by SBS (Seoul
Broadcasting Services). In the past, awards were given to entertainers, but
they aren't anymore. It evolved into a celebratory music event.

Example)
It's the end of the year again… I am sad that I am getting older but happy
because I can see all my Oppa's at the *Gayo Daejeon!*.

거짓말 Geo Jit Mal
(gŏ-jin-mal)

Noun. "Lie"
The mother of all evil. This is probably the single most frequently used
term in melo K-Dramas involving a love triangle because it starts the
entangled love line (without this, there would be no drama!).

Example)
Jinhee: I swear to god I didn't eat your cake!

Bonnie: *Geo jit mal…* What's that on your lip?
Jinhee: It's just some whipping cream that somehow got there. It happens to everybody!

금수저 Geum Soojeo
(gŭm-su-jŏ)

Noun. "Someone Born with Privileges"
Literal meaning is "gold spoon and chopsticks", but is used to describe someone who was born with privileges/perks, for example, extreme wealth coming from wealthy parents. Its English counterpart phrase is "born with a silver spoon in your mouth". It also refers to an unfair advantage which one didn't earn but was inherited.

Example)
Layla: I really want to beat up that new girl…
Sam: Maybe you shouldn't.
Layla: Why?
Sam: She is a *geum soojeo* with a strong backing!
Layla: All right. I will let her slide then.

급 Geup
(gŭp)

Prefix. "All of a Sudden"
Attached to the beginning of a noun, it is used to add a sense of urgency or unexpectedness.

Example)
Lad: Pack your bags! We are going to Hawaii today!
Gal: Oh wow, this is one geup trip!

GG

Chat Acronym. "Submission" "Give Up"
An abbreviation for "good game", it is used in online games as a means to (cyber) shake hands at the end of a match. At the same time, if the losing

side says this first, then it is considered equivalent to admitting defeat. In MMA (Mixed Martial Arts), it is synonymous with "tapping out".

Example)
Girlfriend: Tell me exactly what you did last night! Why was your phone off? Do you want to die?
Boyfriend: *GG…*

기사 Gi Sa
(gi-sa)

Noun. "News Article"
Something that can make or break a celebrity. If a negative reporter writes a nasty article about someone, it can seriously damage and potentially end a celebrity's career. Conversely, a good PR campaign, consisting of a series of well-written articles, can make a struggling entertainer an overnight media darling.

Example)
Jong: Did you see that *gi sa*? Maxus signed a deal with JIK entertainment.
Woo: Yeah I did, but the journalist who wrote it is infamous for delivering false rumors.

GIFs

Noun. "Short Animated Clip"
A short animated clip often containing funny or sexy moments of idols such as bloopers or dance moves. It is termed so because the clip is created in the form of a GIF (Graphics Interchange Format).

Example)
Hey, there is a site where you can see a whole bunch of *GIFs*! I am using one of those in my signature section at the K-Pop forum.

긴장 Gin Jang
(gin-jang)

Noun. "Tension", "Nervousness"
For KPOP fans, it is the feeling you get before the dae sang ("grand prize") is announced.

Example)
Oh my god… This is my first time to see my Oppa's in person! I am so 'Gin Jang'-ing right now.

걸크러쉬 Girl Crush

Noun. "Intense, Non-homo, Liking or Admiration Which a Girl Develops Towards a Person of Same Sex"
An emotional reaction that occurs when the targeted subject possesses the values/characteristics to which the admirers aspire.

Example)
Carolyn: Tiffany is so adorable! Her voice is impeccable and she can play 3 instruments… She is just perfect!
Rana: Are you in love with her?
Carolyn: No, I'm 100% straight. She is just a *girl crush*

고소미 Go So Mi
(go-so-mi)

Noun. "To Sue"
Actually the name of a biscuit snack cracker, but the word "고소" *goso* means "to sue", so people (usually teens) use it instead for fun.

Example)
Yoo: LOL! I left a dirty comment on her picture on Facebook.
Vince: Be careful! You can get a *go so mi* for that.

갓 God
(gat)

Noun. "The One and Only" or "The Omnipotent"
When used in combination with another subject/object, it is converted into the superlative form which implies that it is the absolute best and untouchable. If your bias has a talent in a certain field, you add this term before their name.

Example)
Robert: Wow… Tyler is so good at playing chess. I bet no one in our school can beat him.
Kim: Yup! We should call him *God*-Tyler!
Robert: All hail *God*-Tyler!

고구마 Gogooma
(go-gu-ma)

Noun. Adjective. "Slow-Witted Person/Frustrating Situation"
Literal meaning is "sweet potato", but it is used to describe a very time-consuming situation or someone who is insensitive or slow-witted. Eating sweet potatoes without drinking a beverage causes similar feelings of serious congestion in your chest.

Example)
Seol: I really hate that new K-Drama!
Jin: Why? You've been watching it every week.
Seol: The story just won't develop! It's been like that for 2 months… It's a *gogooma* drama…

Golden Disk Awards

Noun. "Prestigious Annual Awards Show"
A prestigious annual awards show founded in 1986 that is presented by the Music Industry Association of Korea for outstanding achievements in the music industry in South Korea.

Example)

My Oppa has all-killed the K-Pop charts three times this year. I bet he can finally win a grand award at the *Golden Disk Awards* this year!

고마워 Gomawo
(go-ma-wŏ)

Phrase. "Thank You (informal)"
An informal way of saying "thank you". Adding "yo" at the end makes it semi-formal.

Example)
Fan girl: Oppa! We really enjoyed your fan service! *Gomawoyo!*
Ido: My pleasure. *Gomawo* everyone!

공홈 Gong Home
(gong-hom)

Noun. "Official Homepage"
An abbreviation for "공식" *gong sik* ("official") "홈페이지" homepage. It is used when there are many social media (SNS) outlets available so that one knows where to go for official updates/announcements. It is usually the homepage of the entertainment company which your bias belongs to.

Example)
Rabab: Yes! HEXO just announced their come back!
Jihoon: Bull crap! Where did you hear that?
Rabab: On their *gong home*!
Jihoon: Dang... Then it must be real!

공식/비공식 Gong sik/Bi Gong Sik
(gong-shik/pi-gong-shik)

Noun. "Official/Unofficial"
A term used to explain that something is authentic and recognized by an authoritative entity.

Example)

Monica: Yes! I just won a ticket to our oppa's concert!
Hyeri: Really? Where did you get it from?
Monica: Um… Fanclubs.com?
Hyeri: That is not a *gong sik* fan club site. It might be a hoax.

공연 Gong Yeon
(gong-yŏn)

Noun. "Concert", "Recital"
Either a paid event (e.g., Dream Concert) or a public event (e.g., a guerrilla concert)

Example)
I went to see my Oppa's *gong yeon* yesterday. Their live performance was something out of this world.

군대리아 Goondaeria
(gun-dae-ri-a)

Noun. "Hamburger Distributed to Soldiers in the Army as a Military Ration"
A compound word made up of "군대" *goon dae* ("army") + "롯데리아" "lotteria" (a hamburger franchise). It is nothing fancy, really basic compared to those sold at restaurants, so it is often used to describe/make a joke of poor treatment received in the army. If your boy bias joins the army, this is something he will be eating (in tears).

Example)
Girlfriend: Hey honey, come try this I made for you.
Boyfriend: Nom nom nom.
Girlfriend: How does it taste?
Boyfriend: Reminds me of *goondaeria*…
Girlfriend: That… bad?

궁예 Goong Ye
(gung-ye)

Noun. `"Mind Reading"`
Originated from the name of a character in a Korean historical drama
"Taejo Wang Geon", where *Goong Ye*, a Buddhist monk who claimed
himself capable of reading others' minds. Since then, his name has become
synonymous with "mind reading", and it is often used to call out someone
who is nosy and pretends to know everything.

Example)
Eddie: I know what you are thinking. You want to ask that girl out but you
are afraid. Don't be a coward.
Nick: Stop *goong ye*'ing me man, and you are wrong. I'm gay.

궁디팡팡 Goongdi Pang Pang
(gung-di-p'ang-p'ang)

Noun. `"Spanking One's Bottoms"`
A compound word made up of "궁디" *goong di*, a dialect for "hips,
buttocks, ass" and "팡팡" *pang pang*, an adverb describing spanking
sounds. Contrary to common usage, it is not used for corporal punishment,
but as a compliment after doing something praiseworthy.

Example)
Yuri: Our Oppa's just won the Golden Disk Award!
Miso: Awesome! They deserve some *goongdi pang pang* from me!

고수 Gosu
(go-su)

Noun. `"Highly Skilled Person"`
A compound word made up of two Chinese words "고" *go* ("high") and "
수" *su* (or soo) "a move (as in a chess game)" = "master player who knows
many moves". It became a popular term among online gamers
around the world, thanks to the ubiquitous Korean gamers who

contributed to the burgeoning of world's largest e-sports (Starcraft, LOL, Counter Strike, and etc.) leagues. It is the opposite of "초보"

Example)
Juno: Wow, did you know that Jackie Kid has a black belt in Tae Kwon Do?
Mira: I didn't know he was such a *gosu* in martial arts!

게릴라 콘서트 Guerilla Concert

Noun. "Unannounced Surprised Concert"
Originally from MBC's variety TV show "일요일 일요일 밤에" *Ilyoil Ilyoil Bam Ae* ("Sunday, Sunday Night"), where the singer(s) are given just one hour to promote their event in the street, with the goal of attracting an audience of over 5,000. Once the time is up, the singer(s) are blindfolded on the stage, and nervously wait as the numbers are tallied up. If it is less than 5,000, the concert is automatically canceled. Ever since then it has been used to refer to any kind of unannounced concert event usually taking place on the street (including busking and fan service activities).

Example)
Charlie: I just saw AOB singing at the super market!
Jennifer: Holy cow! They must be having a *guerilla concert*! Why didn't you call me?

관종 Gwan Jong
(gwan-jong)

Noun. "Attention Whore"
An abbreviation for "관심 *gwan shim* ("attention") "종자" *jong ja* ("kind/race")". This is somebody who incessantly seeks approval/validation from others. Some are obsessed with social media such as Facebook and Instagram and will go as far as making up stories just to get "likes"; giving "likes" is like feeding them.

Example)
Gyuri: Hey, you really went to that party? I saw your Facebook check-in.
Wonmi: Not really… I just fake-checked-in to get some likes, why not?
Gyuri: You are the biggest *gwan jong* I've ever seen…

괜찮아 Gwenchana
(gwaen-ch'a-na)

Expression. "It's Okay"
Also something you say to mask your true emotions (anger, sadness, surprise, and etc.).

Example)
Hyoa: Ouch! I bumped my head against the window *cry*.
Min: *Gwenchana?*
Hyoa: It really hurts… but did our Oppa's see that?
Min: I don't think so.
Hyoa: *Gwenchana*, then!

귀척 Gwi Cheok
(gwi-ch'ŏk)

Noun. "Pretending to Be Cute"
An abbreviation of "귀여운" *gwi yeo woon* ("cute") "척" *cheok* ("pretending"), which refers to "acting cutesy and coquettish".

Example)
Sonya: Bbuing bbuing~ Oppa~ Aren't I so cute?
Adam: Stop the *gwi cheok*. Aren't you a little too old for that?

귀차니즘 Gwichanism
(gwi-ch'a-ni-jŭm)

Noun. "Annoyance"
A closely translated Konglish counterpart would be "lazism", where one feels annoyed or bothered by almosto everything that is presented before you. This is something a fanboy/fangirl would experience after their bias goes into hiatus. They lose the motivation to live and this feeling of extreme annoyance kicks in.

Example)
Michael: Ugh… I'm so hung over…

Mom: Michael, can you take out the trash?
Michael: I can't.. My religion prohibits it.
Mom: What? What religion?
Michael: *Gwichanism.*

귀요미 Gwiyomi
(gwi-yo-mi)

Noun. "Cutie"
A Korean slang for "a cute and adorable person"

Example)
Awwwww when my Oppa was a little baby, he was such a *gwiyomi!*

해장 Hae Jang
(hae-jang)

Noun. "Easing a Hangover"
A compound word made up of two Chinese words "해" *hae* ("to ease") and
"장" *jang* ("intestine"). It refers to the act of eating food that has soothing
properties, such as *seollong tang* (ox bone soup) and *boogeo gook* (dried
pollock soup), but ramyun is probably the most sought after hangover cure.

Example)
Doug: Holy *burp* molly *hic* I can still taste alcohol in my mouth.
Danny: Me *burp* too. Let's go get some cheese burgers for *hae jang.*

핵 Haek
(haek)

Prefix. "Super"
Its literal meaning is "nuclear", but derived from the word "핵폭탄" *haek
pok tan* ("nuclear bomb"), it is used by the younger generation as an an
adjective to make something the absolute superlative (because the nuclear
bomb is the deadliest of all). Some of the common examples include "
핵노잼" *haek no jam* ("absolute boredom") and "핵피곤" *haek
pi gon* ("utter exhaustion").

Example)
Kimmy: LOL! I accidentally went into a men's restroom and no one noticed it.
Robert: That is not just funny. That is *haek* funny!

행쇼 Haeng Syo
(hang-syo)

Interjection. `"Peace Out"`
A shortened word of the phrase "행복하십쇼" *haeng bok ha sip syo* which means "be happy". It has become very popular ever since G-Dragon started saying it on TV. It can be casually used for saying goodbye, and can be translated as "peace out" in English.
Example)
My fans, it was a great pleasure having you today. Thank you so much and... *Haeng Syo*!

한류 Hallyu
(hal-lyu)

Noun. `"Korean Wave"`
"The Korean Wave". It is the global phenomenon of Korean entertainment and popular culture spreading over the world, through KPOP music, K-Dramas, TV shows, and movies.

Example)
I thought *Hallyu* didn't exist, but every time I travel overseas, I happen to bump into a K-Pop fan.

한복 Hanbok
(han-bok)

Noun. `"Traditional Korean Outfit"`
The traditional outfit of the Korean people. It is often worn on traditional holidays like Chuseok (Harvest Festival) and Seollal (Korean New Year), as well as festive events like weddings. It is characterized by vibrant colors and simple lines. All characters in Sageuk (Korean historical drama) wear

these.

Example)
Tony: Is that Kimono Wonhee's wearing?
Mina: Nope, it's called *Hanbok.*
Tony: Woah, she looks doubly beautiful in it…

합격 Hap Gyuk
(hap-kyŏk)

Noun. "Passing a Test", "Acceptance"
Success in exams, interviews and the like.

Example)
Kimmy, how did the audition go? *Hap Gyuk?*

힐링 Healing

Noun. "Alleviating (Mental) Stress"
Whenever you engage in an activity with the goal of easing the (mostly mental) pain/stress you are in, you use this term, as a noun or an adjective. The term became popular thanks to SBS's hit TV Show "Healing Camp", where guests are invited to openly pour out their troubles to the panels and unburden themselves.

Example)
Joann: I just can't get over the fact our oppa's going to the army… It is the saddest day of my life.
Hanna: We should definitely go on a *healing* trip.

헬조선 Hell Joseon
(hel-cho-sŏn)

Noun. "Horrible Socioeconomic State of South Korea"
A self-deprecating satirical term coined around 2015 by the younger generation who are fed up with and feel hopeless about the current socioeconomic state of South Korea, where the unemployment rate is high and working conditions are sub par, which clearly reflects social inequality

and class stratification.

Example)
Myungsoo: I applied to 30 different job openings and got 0 response.
Doug: Welcome to *Hell Jose*on, man. It is what everyone is going through at this moment.

허당 Heo Dang
(hŏ-dang)

Noun. "Miss Shot"
A Gangwon province dialect for "miss shot" which is used metaphorically to describe someone who looks immaculate but is actually clumsy and incapable. Lee Seung Ki is best known for his Heo Dang character in 2 Days & 1 Night.

Example)
Gyuho looks so smart but it turns out that is such a *heo dang*. He totally flunked the beginner's Korean class.

허접 Heo Jeob
(hŏ-jŏp)

Noun. "Sloppy", "Lousy"
A reference to someone who talks too much and exaggerates their abilities but cannot back up their claims. It can also refer to someone who looks capable, but proves otherwise through (pathetically) poor performances in areas where they were expected to excel.

Example)
Sally: That new transfer student guy turned out to be a total *heo jeob*!
Tony: Why?
Sally: Well he's tall as hell, but when we played basketball yesterday, he plays like a sloth.

허세 Heo Se
(hŏ-se)

Noun. "Bluff"
A compound word made up of two Chinese words "허" *heo* ("empty")
and "세" *se* ("strength"). It refers to the act of showing off courage or
confidence in order to impress others.

Example)
Mike: I will buy that Prada suit and Gucci shoes. Just put them on my
credit card.
Employee: Sir, the credit card is declined.
Rachel: Ha! You and your *heo se*…!

흑기사 Heuk Gi Sa
(hŭk-ki-sa)

Noun. "Man Taking Penalty Shots for a Woman in a Drinking Game"
Literally meaning "Black Knight", it is someone who solves a difficult
situation for a woman, but mostly used in drinking games. The woman who
is saved by "흑기사" owes him a favor and has to fulfill one request he
demands.

Example)
Everyone: Shot! Shot! Shot! Shot! Shot!
Mary: I can't take it anymore. I drank too much already… Does anyone want
to volunteer to be my *heuk gi sa* ?

흑장미 Heuk Jang Mi
(hŭk-chang-mi)

Noun. "Woman Taking Penalty Shots for a Woman in a Drinking Game"
Literally meaning "Black Rose", it is exclusively used in drinking games. It
is the female equivalent of "흑기사".

Example)
Minkyu: Ugh… I lost again?
Brianne: Hey baby, I can be your *heuk jang mi* and take that shot for you. In return, you will have to kiss me!
Minkyu: I would rather die from alcohol poisoning.

흙수저 Heuk Soo Jeo
(hŭk-su-jŏ)

Noun. "Someone Born Without Any Privileges"
A term that makes a contrasts sharply to the word "금수저" *geum soo jeo* (gold spoon and chopsticks). Literally meaning "clay spoon = 흙" *heuk* (clay) + "수저" *soo jeo* (spoon and chopsticks)", it refers to someone who was born without any competitive/comparative advantage over other peers. Hence, they are the low man on the totem pole.

Example)
Dennis: Hey, what are you doing this Friday?
Vince: Work, work, and work!
Dennis: Dang… do you have to work that much?
Vince: *Heuk soo jeo*'s like me have to work our asses off to survive, man.

호모 인턴스 Homo Interns

Noun. "Young Job Seekers Who Are in the Vicious Cycle of Endless Internships"
A satirical term describing the hardships which young Korean job pplicants face. It refers to a vicious cycle of looking for a full-time job but having to settle for an internship position which is often unpaid. It is often likened to the life of KPOP trainees, where they have to spend countless hours with the goal of one day making a debut, which, of course, is never guaranteed.

Example)
5 years and 10 internships. They are called *homo interns*.

Honey Thighs

Noun. "Nice Set of Thighs"
A nice set of thighs that are neither too fat or too skinny. The term "honey" is used figuratively to mean "best".

Example)
I am doing 200 squats everyday so I can have *honey thighs* like Jimin!

후배 Hoobae
(hubae)

Noun. "Junior in a Certain Field"
It refers to a junior who is less experienced or with less seniority in a certain field, regardless of age.

Example)
Although Kyuho is 3 years older than me, he is my *hoobae* because I debuted 2 years before him.

Hook Song

Noun. "Addictive Song"
A very addictive song that gets stuck in your head. It usually has repetitive lyrics or melodies that are catchy.

Example)
I got the beats inside my head and can't get it out of there! Such a strong *hook song* they came out with.

훈남/훈녀 Hoon Nam/ Hoon Nyeo
(hun-nam/hun-nyŏ)

Noun. "Charming Male/Female"
Someone whose charm literally warms the heart of the people around them, due to their attractive looks, but largely because of their inner beauty such

as kindness and thoughtfulness.

Example)
That guy who helped an old lady cross the road is not only kind but handsome! A true example of *Hoon Nam.*

헐 Hul
(hŏl)

Interjection. "Whoa"
Something you say when you are dumbfounded or lost for words.

Example)
Oyu: Layla, I accidentally spilled coffee on your Oppa's picture…
Layla: *Hul…*

헌팅 Hunting

Noun. "To Pick up"
A Koreanized English expression used to refer to the act of making a casual acquaintance and asking someone for their contact information to schedule a date.

Minu: Hey! Let's go for some *hunting*!
James: Right on! Let me go grab my rifles.
Minu: WTH are you doing?
James: You said we are going hunting!
Minu: No, dude! I meant picking up chicks!

현질 Hyeon Jil
(hyŏn-jil)

Noun. "Buying Video Game Items With Cash"
The easiest and quickest way to upgrade your cyber game character. In many mobile games, the game developers let the users download the game for free, but offer in-app purchases for those who wish to buy items with cash. Because it would take too much time to earn that item/reach a certain

level, many people make an "investment" and seek instant gratification.

Example)
Oyu: Look at my character! It's got max attack and max defense!
Byeon: How? You just started playing yesterday.
Oyu: *Hyeon jil* is the answer, buddy!
Byeon: You know you could have bought a new car with all the money you spent online, right?

현웃 Hyeon Woot
(hyŏ-nut)

Noun. "Laughing in Reality"
Contrary to LOL (Laughing Out Loud or "ㅋㅋㅋ"), which is the biggest lie on the Internet, the reader finds it so funny and hilarious that they burst out laughing in real life.

Example)
Daeho: LOL! Mina just farted while giving a presentation.
Max: LOL! I just had a *hyeon woot*. She must have been so embarrassed.

형 Hyung
(hyŏng)

Noun. "Older Brother"
A term used by a younger male to address an older male sibling. It can be used for any older male who they share enough emotional intimacy with. Sometimes the older male won't let the younger male call him this, unless permission is given. It can be used in place of someone's name.

Example)
Hey, Tony, meet my little brother. Since he is 2 years older than you, he is your *hyung*.

형님 Hyungnim
(hyŏng-nim)

Noun. "Older Brother (honorific)"
An honorific term for "Hyung", where "nim" can be translated as "sir" or "Mr.", and the bosses of 조폭 *jopok* (Korean mafia) are also called this.

Example)
Insoo: Hyung! Can I use your computer?
Inho: Only if you call me *hyungnim.*

Hyungwhore

Noun. "Person Who Loves to Hang Out with His Hyungs a Lot"
A male KPOP idol who is always seen in the company of *hyungs* (older males). It does not mean that he is homosexual, but it is what he likes doing. Usually, the maknae members of a group show this tendency.

Example)
Yuno always hangs out with his hyungs. Many thought he might be gay, but he also has a girlfriend. So with that possibility ruled out, he is just a *hyungwhore.*

이불킥 I Bool Kick
(i-bul-k'ik)

Noun. "Kicking Oneself"
A compound word made up of "이불" *i bool* ("comforter") + "킥" (kick) = "kicking one's comforter". It refers to a situation where someone is lying in bed, waiting to fall asleep, and all of a sudden something embarrassing they did in the past flashes through their mind, and they kick the comforter out of shame.
Example)
Maya: Remember the dude who threw up in front of everyone at band camp last year?
Jody: Yeah! I bet he is still *i bool kicking* til today!

이열치열 I Yeol Chi Yeol
(i-yŏl-ch'i-yŏl)

Phrase. <mark>"Eating Samgyetang on a Super Hot Korean Summer Day"</mark>
A four-letter Chinese idiom meaning "fighting fire with fire", which refers to the act of consuming boiling-hot, rejuvenating, stamina-restoring, and nutritious soups like Samgyetang (chicken soup with ginseng) to beat the summer heat, usually during "boknal", the dog days of Korea's summer.

Example)
Nana: Hot! Hot!
Wongyo: What is that you are eating?
Nana: Oh, this is samgyetang. So hot!
Wongyo: Damn, why don't you get something cold, like ice cream?
Nana: No, this is called *i yeol chi yeol*! Our way of beating the summer heat!

Idol

Noun. <mark>"Young KPOP Entertainer"</mark>
Young KPOP entertainers who have come through many years of vigorous training in multiple areas, including singing, acting, dancing, and entertaining on TV shows. They work either as a solo artist or as a group, or often as both interchangeably.

Example)
Tim: Okay, so is Felix an *idol*?
Max: No way, I know that he can sing, but he is in his 30's and have no talent in other things…

Idolization

Noun. <mark>"Dramatic Change or Transformation of Appearance (for the better)"</mark>
A dramatic change or transformation of appearance for the better, mostly through weight loss, hair styles, or even plastic surgery, thereby earning the "idol" status.

Example)
After losing 25kg, Aya became a totally different person, from ajumma to idol! What an *idolization* it is.

익게 Ik Ge
(ik-ke)

Noun. "Anonymous Bulletin Board"

An abbreviation for "익명" *ik myeong* ("anonymous") + "게시판" *ge si pan* ("bulletin board"). Unlike its intended purpose to facilitate the exchange of honest opinions, it often turns into the incubator for numerous fan wars.

Example)
Marcus: Chris! You are in big trouble, my man!
Chris: What? Why?
Marcus: Why did you write that post talking trash about your ex?
Chris: Huh? I did... but I did it in the *ik ge* section...
Marcus: Man... there is no *ik ge* in our forum! You must have confused it with something else.

일진 Il Jin
(il-chin)

Noun. "School Gangs"

A group of school bullies (mostly in high school) who engage in violent and even criminal activities against weaker/vulnerable classmates. This is a serious social issue, and some idols/celebs have been severely criticized, as their past history as school gang members have been disclosed after their debut.
Example)
Fiora: Did you hear that Wendy was a notorious *il jin* in high school?
Vera: No way, with such innocent face?

인강 In Gang
(in-'gang)

Noun. `"Online Lectures"`
An abbreviation for "인터넷" (Internet) "강의" *gang eui* ("lecture"), a convenient means of acquiring knowledge among the younger generation. Many Internet-based companies offer courses to their subscribers.
Example)
Murielle: My desire for learning is insatiable, but I have no time to go to school!
Yura: Hey, just take *in gang* at home then!

인지도 In Ji Do
(in-ji-do)

Noun. `"(Brand) Awareness"`
A tool to gauge the level of brand awareness of something (i.e., a product, a political campaign, a celebrity, etc.) For KPOP fans, there are many factors used to gauge this, including chart rankings, the number of views on YouTube, the number of members of a fan club, etc. But the easiest method is taking the subway and see if anyone recognizes them.

Example)
Hello Mini went out for a walk in a crowded park, but no one recognized her. She was slightly bothered by her low *in ji do*.

인사 In Sa
(in-sa)

Noun. `"Showing Respect"`
The literal meaning is "greetings", but it has more subtle nuances. In Korean society, age plays an important role in determining someone's place in the social hierarchy, there are rules of politeness, and "인사" is one of them. It is more than making a bow, it includes keeping in touch with and looking after someone older or a superior at work, which all boils down to a matter of showing respect.

Example)
In sa, or showing respect to sunbae's, is the most important element for a good reputation.

인기 Inki
(in-'gi)

Noun. "Popularity"
A reference to the degree of popularity of an idol, measured by various tools such as the number of TV/Radio appearances, the size of a fan club, etc.

Example)
Jinpyo has so many friends. His *inki* knows no limit.

인기가요 Inkigayo
(in-'gi-ga-yo)

Noun. "Popular KPOP Songs", "Music Program by SBS"
A music program by SBS which airs every Sunday, featuring live performances by the hottest and the most popular artists. This is a popular TV show in which the singers make a "comeback stage".

Example)
Tune to channel 5! It's time for *Inkigayo*! Brothers are having a comeback stage today!

입덕 Ip Deok
(ip-tŏk)

Noun. "Getting Hooked on an Idol"
An abbreviation for a compound word made up of "입" *ip* ("to enter") " 덕후" deok hu ("otaku" - geek/mania)" which refers to the very moment one falls for an idol. This syndrome commonly afflicts someone watching a video clip of an idol which engulfs the "off-guard" audience with "visual attack (handsomeness/cuteness overload)"

Example)
Mindy: When was your *ip deok* moment, Jen?
Jen: Oh, when his music video really wowed me.

자삭 Ja Sak
(ja-sak)

Noun. "Self Censorship"
An abbreviation for "자진" *ja jin* ("self/voluntary") + "삭제" *sak je*
("deletion"). It is the act of someone deleting their already uploaded post/
photo/file. The decision is usually made after 1) receiving feedback from
other users 2) belatedly realizing its nappropriateness/awkwardness.

Example)
Ikhyeon: Wow! I've got so many comments on my post!
Rory: What are people saying?
Ikhyeon: They are all telling me to *ja sak*...

재방송 Jae Bang Song
(jae-bang-song)

Noun. "Rerun"
A compound word made up of "재" jae ("re/repeat") + "방송" bang song
("airing, broadcast"). K-Drama fans who missed a live airing of an episode
have to settle for this and try t cover their ears before they finish watching
the episode to avoid a spoiler.

Example)
Slow Dude: Goooooooooooooooooooooooooal! Korea scores! Oh my god!
Less Slow Dude: Dude, chill down, that's a jae bang song... they lost the
game...
Slow Dude: Oh.

잼 Jaem
(jaem)

Noun. "Fun", "Interest"

Kids' and teenagers' way of saying the word "재미" *jae mi* ("fun, interest"). It is used in conjunction with other adjectives (e.g., "빅" big "잼" jaem "fun" - "Much Fun", "노 no 잼" "No Fun". It is a very effective conversation-ender.

Example)
Randy: Do you want to hear a joke? One time…
Jayna: No thanks, your jokes are *no jam*.

자기 Jagi
(ja-gi)

Noun. "Sweetheart"

Can be used by married/unmarried couples.

Example)
Jagi~ Tomorrow is our three year anniversary. Don't forget!

Jailbait

Noun. "Bias Who is Under 18"

The danger of falling in love with an idol who is under the age of 18, which is the legal age in Korea. It became a popular term when Taemin of SHINee debuted when he was only 16 back in 2008, which led to countless noona fans falling in love with him.

Example)
The reason why the Mircale Kids are called the "*jailbait* band" is because their average age is just 13.

작업 Jak Eop
(ja-gŏp)

Noun. "To Flirt With Somebody"
Literally means "operation" or "work", but is used figuratively to refer to the act of trying to attract someone, mostly for amusement rather than with serious intentions.

Example)
Rule #1 – Don't *jak eop* on a girl who has a boyfriend.

잘자 Jalja
(jal-ja)

Phrase. "Good Night"
It is a sweet conversation-ender when talking to your loved one on the phone at night.

Example)
Yawn I feel so sleepy now. I'm going to bed early today. *Jalja* everybody~!

제발 Jebal
(jae-bal)

Phrase. "Please"
Something you say when you want something dearly.

Example)
Dear god, *jebal* help our Oppa's win the award!

Jeju Island

Noun. "Beautiful Island in the Southernmost Part of Korea"
A beautiful island in the southernmost part of Korea. It is a top vacation destination not only for Koreans but for many foreigners visiting Korea. In

K-Dramas, rich male characters often take females characters there, either to have an intimate time or to impress them.

Example)
Why do all the couples in K-Dramas have their first encounter in *Jeju Island*?

즐 Jeul
(jŭl)

Phrase. "Whatever"
A term derived from an adjective "즐거운" *jeul geo un* ("fun, entertaining"), which is used in expressions like "즐거운 게임 하세요 *jeul geo un game ha se yo* ("have a good game"). The shortened term, however, has evolved to become a conversation-ender. By saying즐 to someone, you express your intention of not wanting to engage in any further conversation with the person, similar to saying "Have a Great Day, Sir.".

Example)
Rex: Mimi! You know what you look like? A racoon! LOL
Mimi: *Jeul*!

지못미 Ji Mot Mi
(ji-mon-mi)

Noun. "Sorry I Couldn't Save You"
An abbreviation for "지켜주지 못해" *ji kyeo joo ji mot hae* (that I couldn't save you) "미안해" *mi an hae* ("sorry"). It is mainly used when someone looks funny (i.e., ugly funny) in a picture (e.g., a snap shot capturing an ugly moment). You are sorry because you 1) couldn't take a better picture 2) weren't available to Photoshop it 3) just feel sorry that the person is ugly. You can also use this in drinking games when someone has to drink shots as a penalty for losing a game.

Example)
Hailey: LOL! Daniel looks like a sloth in this photo.
Xavier: *Ji mot mi* Daniel…

지름신 Ji Reum Shin
(ji-rŭm-shin)

Noun. **"Impulse Buying"**
A compound word made up of "지름" *ji reum* ("impulse buying") + "신" *shin* ("god") = "god of impulse buying". People use this imaginary deity as a scapegoat to put the blame on for their lack of willpower (uncontrollable impulsiveness) as if their buying decision was the result of an unavoidable act of God (divine intervention). They usually come to their senses upon receipt of their credit card statement.

Example)
Sarah: Ben! Did you really buy this $3,000 bicycle with my card?
Ben: No I didn't. *Ji reum shin* did.

집 Jib
(jip)

Noun. **"Group's Full Length Album", "Home"**
A term for 1) A group's full-length album, which usually contains upwards of 10 songs, while other works contain less than that (i.e., "mini album", "digital single", and etc.). 2) "Home".

Example)
Mr. A's 8th *jib* had 18 tracks and many other bonus materials.

직찍 Jik Jjik
(jik-tchik)

Phrase. **"Photo/Video Taken by Me"**
An abbreviation for "직접" *jik jeop* ("in person") "찍음" *jjik eum* ("taking"). For celeb shots, it is a product of truly zealous fans' passion as they for days and days to get a glimpse of their bias, or it is the result of pure luck. You can also use this for any photo/video you have taken in person and you have all the rights pertaining to the final material.

Example)

Keira: Check out this photo, girls!
Judy: Wow! Is this a *jik jjik?*
Keira: Yup! I went to our oppa's concert and took in myself.

진상 Jin Sang
(jin-sang)

Noun. "Eyesore"
Someone who has a nasty temper and makes a fuss over the most trivial
things. It is similar to "drama queen" but it mostly refers to customers who
demand outrageous favors (e.g., forcing the store to accept a return of a
non-returnable product) because they believe they are the boss.

Example)
Joohee was screaming and even pushing the poor restaurant server over a
strand of hair found in her meal. No one knew that she could be such a *jin
sang*.

짜가 Jja Ga
(tcha-ga)

Noun. "Counterfeit" "Knock Off"
"가짜" *ga jja* ("fake") spelled backward, but it is most often used to refer
to a counterfeit product.

Mingyu: *Bling Bling* Look at ma Lorex!
Juno: You mean Rolex?
Mingyu: LOL it is Lorex cause it is a *jja ga*, my man!

짱 Jjang (Zzang)
(tchang)

Noun. "The Best" "Awesome" "Incredible"
A word which appeared among the younger population in the 1990's, it has
been widely used among all generations recently. It is not, however, used in
formal/official settings such as TV news.

Example)
My son got straight A's! My son *Jjang*!
My Oppa just showed off his dancing skills. *Jjang*!

찌질이 Jji Jil I
(tchi-ji-ri)

Noun. "Nerd", "Loser"
Used to describe someone who is good-for-nothing, worthless, or pathetic.
In K-Drama settings, these characters often turn into a "winner", often
through a major overhaul that awakens the inner hero (e.g., getting
humiliated by their crush, or a near-death experience).

Example)
Teddy: Do you like Spiderman?
Kim: No… he is a *jji jil i* when not in his spandex.

찌라시 Jji Ra Shi
(tchi-ra-shi)

Noun. "Tabloid"
A style of journalism which focuses on sensational topics (i.e., vivid
crime stories, celebrity gossip and junk food news) in order to distinguish
themselves from other media. Although often criticized for overly
sensational topics, they always find a significant share of readers who
appreciate the stories that can't be found elsewhere.

Example)
According to a *jji ra shi* circulating on the Internet, the youngest member
of group VODKA sleeps with his thumb in his nose.

좋아요 Jo A Yo
(jo-a-yo)

Phrase. "Like"
It refers to the "like" or "heart" button on Facebook and Instagram, which
serves as a self-esteem booster for many.

Example)
Some people believe that a post that receives less than 10 *jo a yo*'s is a shame.

조공 Jo Gong
(jo-gong)

Noun. "Giving Gifts to One's Bias"
Original meaning is "tribute", but in KPOP lingo, it refers to the act of giving gifts to a bias.
Example)
June made his *jo gong* to his favorite member of the girl group 4 Wonders through the fan club, but he is not sure if it will ever make it to her.

조낸 Jo Naen
(jo-naen)

Adjective. "Friggin'"
Originated from a typo of "좃내" *jon nae* ("frigging"), an adverb used to emphasize something you say.

Example)
Michael: Ew! It tastes horrible! *Jo naen* horrible!

존대말 Jon Dae Mal
(jon-dae-mal)

Noun. "Formal/Honorific Way of Speaking"
The Korean language has different styles and forms of speaking. It is the polite form in which you basically attach "~요" yo and "~습니다/ㅂ니다" ~seup ni da/~up nida" to the end of a sentence. It is determined by the social hierarchy (age, position at work/school, and etc.)

Example)
Byeongjin: Hey man, gomawo!
Ronald: Dude, you should use *jon dae mal* to me! I am a hyung to you!
Byeongjin: Oh, sorry. Gomawoyo, hyungnim!

존예/존잘 Jon Ye/Jon Jal
(jon-nye/jon-jal)

Noun. "Pretty/Handsome as Hell"
An abbreviation for "존나" *jon na* ("~as hell") + "예쁘다" *ye peu da* ("pretty") / "잘생겼다" *jal saeng gyeot da* ("handsome/good looking").

Example)
Boyfriend: Honey, I am going to call you *jon ye* from now on. You want to call me *jon jal*?
Girlfriend: Pay me.

주장미 Joo Jang Mi
(ju-jang-mi)

Phrase. "Episode Preview"
An abbreviation for "주요" *joo yo* ("important") "장면" *jang myeon* ("scenes") "미리 보기" *miri bogi* ("to view in advance"). It is a handy feature if you don't have much time to watch a full episode, but it can also be a spoiler.

Example)
Too curious about the ending, but too much homework to do, Jordan watched the *joo jang mi* of the last episode.

JYP

Noun. "Jin Young Park"
These are initials of Jin Young Park, one of Korea's most successful and influential music artist. He is also the president of the entertainment company JYP Nation.

Example)
I like *JYP* as a singer, but more as a business man.

JYP Entertainment

Noun. "One of Big Three Entertainment Companies"

One of the Big Three entertainment companies in Korea. Its artists include Wonder Girls, GOT7, miss A, 2 AM and 2 PM

Example)

Did you know that *JYP Entertainment*'s got itself covered for 24 hours because they have 2 AM and 2 PM?

카톡 Ka Tok
(K'a-t'ok)

Noun. "Messaging App Virtually Used by Every Korean Smartp

It refers to Kakaotalk, a chatting/messaging app that holds the dominant position in Korea. It is the most widely used means of communication today.

Example)

Jim: Call me when you get home, buddy!

Tony: I have no talk minutes. I will *ka tok* you!

칼퇴 Kal Toe
(K'al-t'oe)

Noun. "Leaving Work On Time"

An abbreviation for "칼" *kal* ("knife") "퇴근" *toe geun* ("getting off work"). Literally means "leaving work on time, sharp as a knife". It is what Korean office workers dream of, but in reality, they often find themselves working overnight.

Example)

Being able to *kal twae* is something which all Korean office workers dream of.

감사합니다 Kamsa Hamnhida
(Gamsahamnida)

Phrase. "Thank You (formal)"
Formal way of saying thank you, which is equivalent to saying "I appreciate it."

Example)
Amy met the man who saved her life, but all she could say was "*Kamsa Hamnida*".

케바케 Ke Ba Ke
(K'e-ba-k'e)

Phrase. "Case by Case" "YMMV (Your Mileage May Vary"
An abbreviation of an English phrase, which means "results may vary depending on the situation". It is frequently used with the term 사바사*sa ba sa*. When giving advice to someone, make sure to mention this so you are not held accountable for any unexpected outcomes.

Example)
Michelle: Why did he get the job and I didn't? It's not fair!
Mark: Well, often times who gets the job is *ke ba ke*.

키보드 워리어 Keyboard Warrior

Noun. "Someone Who Expresses Anger/Hate on the Internet"
The individuals who display bad temper through malicious comments, cyber-bullying etc., mainly because they are incapable of doing it in real life and the Internet provides anonymity.

Example)
Getting bullied at school and rejected by a girl, Minu became a *keyboard warrior* who expressed his anger through harsh comments on other's SNS.

김떡순 Kim Tteok Soon
(kim-ttŏk-sun)

Noun. "Kimbab, Tteokbokki, Soondae"
The most popular trio of Korean street foods, so popular that they have are abbreviated to resemble the name of a real person.

Example)
Although Jenny doesn't have a boyfriend, she wouldn't cry because her best friend, *Kim Ddeok Soon*, is always by her side.

김치 Kimchi
(Kim-chi)

Noun. "Staple Korean Food"
A staple of Korean cuisine. Traditional fermented Korean side dish made of vegetables such as baechu (napa cabbage) with a variety of seasonings. The most representative Kimchi is baechu Kimchi. This tangy and spicy fermented side dish made of vegetables with a variety of seasonings has become an inseparable part of the Korean lifestyle, to the point where people view it as part of their identity.

Interjection.
A word you say to induce a smile when taking a picture, similar to saying "cheese" in English.

Example)
You can't say you had Korean food unless you try *Kimchi*!

킹왕짱 King Wang Jjang
(k'ing-wang-tchang)

Interjection. "The Bestest"
A compound word made up of "King + 왕 *wang* ("King") + 짱 *jjang* ("best")". A set of 3 superlatives, thus it is the best possible thing in the entire universe.

Example)
Girlfriend: How much do you love me?
Boyfriend: A lot!
Girlfriend: That's it?
Boyfriend: No, *king wang jjang*!

킹카/퀸카 Kingka / Queenka

Noun. "Male Hottie/Female Hottie"
A male/female hottie who is not only good looking but also rich and well educated.
Example)
I think the *queenka* of group QTQT is Myo. She is from a chaebol family and always gets straight A's in school.

깝 Kkab
(kkap)

Noun. "Acting Crazy and Overly Energetic"
Slang for someone acting crazy and overly energetic to the point where they are thought to be insane. Jo Kwon of 2 AM popularized this term with his outrageous dance moves, earning the name "Kkab Kwon".

Example)
Last night in the club, I saw so many kids doing the *kkab* dance. I am pretty sure they were on something.

깜놀 Kkam Nol
(kkam-nol)

Phrase. "Startled"
An abbreviation for "깜짝 놀라다" *kkam jjak nolada* ("very surprised"). This is the type of response you would have if your favorite bias announced retirement.

Example)
Nina: Mina, can you come pick me up at the hospital…
Mina: Why? What's wrong?

THE KPOP DICTIONARY

Nina: I ran out of taxi money and this is the farthest the driver would take me.
Mina: *Kkam nol*!

꽐라 Kkwal La
(kkwal-la)

Noun. "Wasted"
The state of being wasted. There is a hypothesis that it is related to koala bears because they eat eucalyptus leaves, which is are believed to contain chemicals similar to alcohol. Thereby saying that koala bears are always drunk and spend most of their time sleeping.

Example)
Sam: People call me Koala! I think that is a cute nickname.
Tony: You drunkhead! I bet they meant *Kkwal La*…

콩다방 Kong Da Bang
(k'ong-da-bang)

Noun. "Coffee Bean"
A compound word for "콩" *kong* ("bean") + "다방" *da bang* ("coffee shop, tea house"). This is another large coffee franchise, along with Starbucks, where people willingly spend more for a cup of coffee than they would on lunch.

Example)
Amy: *Kong da bang* at 7 tonight, right?
Doug: What the what?
Amy: Coffee Bean.

콩가루 Kong Ga Ru
(k'ong-ga-ru)

Noun. "Messed Up Family"
Literal meaning is "bean powder family", but is figuratively used to describe a family that is so unstable and fragile that when the air is blown

near it, everything will just fall apart and collapse, just like bean powder. It is one of the most stereotypical families in mak jang (drama with unrealistic and outrageous story lines) K-Dramas.

Example)
Judy comes from a *kong ga ru* family. Her mother has a boyfriend and her dad just went to jail for possession of child pornography.

Leader

Noun. "Idol Member Who is in Charge and Oversees the Group"
A member of an idol group who is in charge of organizing and managing its members. Although not in all cases, the oldest of the members usually takes on this role.

Example)
Awesome Sophomores have 15 members and it is extremely difficult to guess who the *leader* of the group is.

이수만 Lee Soo Man
(i-su-man)

Noun. "The Founder and Chairman of SM Entertainment"
The founder and chairman of SM Entertainment.

Example)
Oh, so SM Entertainment is named after the founder *Lee Soo Man?*

리즈시절 Leeds Si Jeol
(ri-jŭ-shi-jŏl)

Noun. Adjective. "Heyday" "Prime" "One's Best Days"
The time when Ji Sung Park and Alan Smith were teammates at Manchester United (English Premier League Football Club). At that time, Alan Smith wasn't getting many playing opportunities like he did at Leeds United Football Club when he was in his prime. For that reason, "during his days at Leeds" became synonymous with "someone's best days".

Example)
Hector: I keep losing StarCraft matches these days! I miss my *leeds si jeol*…
Enzo: What *leeds si jeol*? You have only won once so far and it was because the opponent got disconnected.

레전설 Legen Seol
(re-jŏn-sŏl)

Noun. "Legendary Figure"
"레전드" legend and "전설" *jeon seol* ("legend") combined as one word to make it sound funny, because "gen" of "legend" and "jeon" of "jeon seol" sound the same.

Example)
After winning all five music charts, which is the first in the music industry, BTBT became a *legen seol*.

립싱크 Lip Sync

Noun. "Pretending to Sing"
The act of pretending to sing while simply matching lip movements to pre-recorded vocals. It is a godsend for many who lack singing talent.

Example)
Ingu failed the audition because he attempted to *lip sync*.

로케 Locae
(ro-k'e)

Noun. "Location Shooting"
The practice of filming in the actual setting or location in which a story takes place rather than on a stage set up to emulate the environments of the actual location.

Example)
The new K-Drama about lovers in Russia was *locae*'d in Moscow.

러브콜 Love Call

Noun. "Offer"
The act of asking someone to appear on a show, or star in a film, CF, or movie.
Example)
Thanks to the recent success of her CF, Shu has been receiving countless *love call*'s.

Love Line

Noun. "Map of Love Relationships Among Characters in"

A map of complicated relationships among characters in a K-Drama. For example, if Soomi and Tak have been having something going on, and finally decide to go out, then they have just formed a *love line*.

Example)
Hey sweetie, do you want to form a *love line* with me?

M Line

Noun. "Chiseled Abs"
A term to describe a chiseled abdominal area of a male body. The highly developed and ripped abdominal area resembles the alphabet M.

Example)
I have been working out for a month now. Do I have *M Line?* Oh no… I still have D Line.

맹구 Maeng Goo
(maeng-gu)

Noun. "Idiot"
The name of a comical character from an extremely popular 90's comedy, best known for his foolishness. Since then, the name has become synonymous with "someone foolish".

Example)
Kim: I just lost $500 at the casino.
Nina: You *maeng goo*! Didn't I tell you that you have no chance of winning against the casino?

막장 Makjang
(mak-jang)

Noun. "K-Drama With Crazy Storylines"

Slang for something that can't get any worse. It is widely used for describing K-Dramas that have seriously outrageous and unrealistic storylines (e.g., birth secrets, adultery, accidents, memory loss, fatal illness, etc.) to the point that it becomes ridiculous. It does, however, attract a significant number of fans, due to its addictive nature, speedy development, and surprising plot twists.

Example)
Dude, you went out with this girl and now you are dating her sister? You are living a *makjang* life!

막내 Maknae
(mak-nae)

Noun. "The Youngest Member of a Group"

The youngest member of an idol group who is often the life of the party. They also assume the role of taking care of little favors and chores for the group.

Example)
Anybody can tell that Grace is the *maknae* of the group because she is the most energetic, innocent, and silly girl of all.

말도안돼 Maldo Andwae
(mal-do-an-dwae)

Phrase. "Nonsense!"
Literally means "does not even make any sense". It can be used as a rejection when somebody asks for an outrageous favor or as an exclamation when something beyond belief actually happens.
Example)
TV: And the winner is… XOLO!
AAA fans: *Maldo andwae*… This award is rigged!

MAMA

Noun. "Mnet Asian Music Awards"
An annual event and one of the major KPOP awards events hosted by CJ E&M through its music channel subsidiary Mnet in which many high-profile actors and celebrities from China, Hong Kong, Japan, and Taiwan also participate.

Example)
This year, *MAMA* will be held in Shanghai, China. I wonder who will win the top award.

만렙 Man Leb
(mal-lep)

Noun. "The Highest Level"
An abbreviation for a compound word of a Chinese word "만" *man* ("full") and an English word "레벨" level, shortened and pronounced as "렙" leb. It refers to someone who has reached the highest status in a field such as an online game. It can also be used to describe someone who is full of "geekiness".
Example)
Jim: Level 99! Level 99! I did it! Yes!
Andrew: Congrats, mate! You just reached *man leb*!

Manner Hands

Noun. "Trying Not to Touch Someone While Taking a Photo Together"

A kind and considerate act where a male's hand stops short, in an attempt to not make contact with a female's shoulders or waist. It is also known as "hover hands" as the hand literally hovers over the area.

Example)
Look how Keegan is doing his *manner hands* while taking pictures with his fans! He looks like a magician.

Manner Legs

Noun. "Lowering Height to Match That of Another"

A kind and considerate act to accommodate height difference. It is usually done by the taller male spreading his legs sideways while standing, thereby lowering himself to achieve a mutually desired goal (e.g., kissing, hugging, and etc.).

Example)
I love it when Jiho does the *manner legs* to kiss her! That's so sweet of him.

맛있어 Mashisso
(ma-shi-ssŏ)

Interjection. "Delicious"

Literally meaning "delicious", but can also be used as an expression of euphoria when eating something that pleases your taste buds.

Example)
Oh my god, did you make this? *Mashisso!*

맞선 Mat Seon
(mat-sŏn)

Noun. "Formal Blind Date Arranged by Parents"
A formal blind date prearranged by the parents. In K-Dramas, parents (usually the rich guy's mother) often use this tactic to break up a relationship because they think the girl (who usually comes from a poor family) is not good enough for their son.

Example)
I think it's about time I got married. My mom set me up for 5 *mat seon's* this month!

마음 Maum
(ma-ŭm)

Noun. "Mind"/"Heart"
It refers to the personality/characteristic which a person is originally born with, but also can mean one's emotions.

Example)
You stole my *maum* and you can have it. I am so in love with you.

Melo

Noun. "Melo Drama"
A gripping K-Drama genre that is full of exciting/sad events and exaggerated/forced acting. It is not limited to love stories, it also includes various topics such as revenge, success, and forgiveness.

Example)
Juno didn't even have two pennies to rub together, but now he is one of the most richest man in town. Listening to his success story is such a *melo* drama.

멜론 Melon

Noun. "Music Streaming Service"
An Internet-based music streaming service where you can listen to music for a fee.

Example)
Mina: How much are you paying for Melon?
Doohee: The fruit or the streaming service?

멘붕 Men Bung
(men-bung)

Noun. "Mental Breakdown"
The psychological state of total chaos, which is caused by something utterly beyond belief.

Example)
I got so *men bung'ed* when I heard my Oppa's been having a secret affair with the member of GBGB.

멘트 Ment

Noun. "Pick up Line"
Originated from the word "comment", but in Korea it refers to something sweet and charming one says to seduce the opposite sex.

Example)
Dohoon: Hey girl, you look like a traffic ticket!
Jenny: Excuse me?
Dohoon: You got FINE written all over you!
Jenny: Is that a *ment*? Don't flirt with me, Mr.!

먹튀 Meok Twi
(mŏk-t'wi)

Noun. "Eat and Run". "Dine and Dash"
Used to describe an overpaid contract, especially in sports where a player shows a poor level of performance after signing a blockbuster contract. In business it refers to an entity that does not fully carry out the mutually agreed terms after signing a contract and securing their share of the money.

Example)
Fing: Hey, can you lend me $50? I will pay back in a week with interest.
Mei: Hell no! I heard you *mweok twi*'ed with Jenny's money last week!

미쳤어 Mi Chyeo Sso
(mi-ch'yŏ-ssŏ)

Phrase. "Crazy"
An expression used to describe various emotions such as surprise, joy, anger, depending on the situation.
Example)
You drank that whole bottle of Soju? *Mi Chyeo Sso*?

미존 Mi Jon
(mi-jon)

Noun. "Scene Stealer"
An abbreviation for "미친" *mi chin* ("crazy") "존재감" *jon jae gam* ("presence"). It refers to someone with an overwhelming swag, who dwarfs everyone around them.

Example)
The movie wouldn't have been complete without him. Yes, he is such a *mi jon* no one else can imitate.

미남/미녀 Mi Nam / Mi Nyeo
(mi-nam/mi-nyŏ)

Noun. "Good Looking Male/Beautiful Female"
A compound word made up of two Chinese words - "미" *mi* means
"beautiful" "남" *nam* means "male" and "녀" *nyeo* means "female".

Example)
Wow, that *mi nyeo is* a real head-turner. She is the most beautiful girl I've
ever seen!

미안해 Mianhae
(mi-an-hae)

Phrase. "Sorry"
Informal way of saying "sorry". It can only be used between people with
emotional intimacy, such as friends and family. An older person can say
this to a younger person if the age difference is wide (e.g., a grandpa to a
grandson). Adding "yo" makes it more formal.

Example)
Oppa, you are no longer my bias… *Mianhae*…

밀당 Mil Dang
(mil-dang)

Noun. "Psychological Tug of War"
A fierce psychological warfare that usually takes place among couples, as
they attempt to protect their ego and in the hope of securing the upper hand
in the relationship. Not everyone is good at playing this game, and if not
played well, the rope can snap and recoil.

Example)
Sabrina: He hasn't called me for 3 days. Should I?
Jim: No, Sabrina – I am 100% sure that he's playing *mil dang* with you.
Don't give in!

민낯 Min Nat
(min-nat)

Noun. "Bare Face"
A face without any make up on. Synonymous with 쌩얼 *saeng eol*.

Example)
Oh hi, who are you? Oh, it's you! Didn't recognize you without any make up on. Your *min nat* is quite different from the picture.

미니 앨범 Mini Album

Noun. "Album that Contains about Half or 1/3 of the Songs of a Full Lengt"
A short album which contains less than 10 songs but more than one (known as a single album). It usually includes remixes and instrumental versions of the songs.

Example)
Nora: When will our oppa's hiatus end? It's been 2 years already.
Nancy: I know, right? They should release a *mini album* or something at least!

미워 Miwo
(mi-wŏ)

Phrase. "Hate You"
A cute way of saying "I hate you".

Example)
Why didn't you call me? Oppa *miwo miwo miwo miwo!*

목소리 Mok So Ri
(mok-so-ri)

Noun. "Voice"
Can also be used figuratively to refer to someone's opinion or assertion.

Kyumin has the sweetest *mok so ri* among all K-Pop singers.

몰카 Mol Ca

Noun. "Hidden Camera"
An abbreviation for "몰래 mol lae ("secretly") + 카메라" ("camera"),
referring to the act of filming someone unbeknownst to theme. The term
originated from MBC's popular comedy TV show "일요일 일요일 밤에
(*Ilyoil Ilyoil Bam Ae* – "Sunday, Sunday Night", where Lee Kyung Kyu,
a famous comedian, set up a hidden camera to see how celebrities would
react to a hilarious situation. Recently, however, the term has been more
frequently used to describe criminal activities, and a handful of celebrities
have fallen victim to such crimes (i.e., leaked sex tape).

Example)
After Jason's *mol ca* on his private life leaked, many of his sponsors
cancelled CF contracts.

몰컴 Mol Com

Noun. "Using Computer Secretly"
An abbreviation for "몰래 *mol lae* ("secretly") 컴퓨터 computer, meaning
secretly using your computer when you are not supposed to (e.g., after
bedtime). You engage in this thrilling activity after you make sure your
parents are fully asleep. During this time, the whirring sound of your
computer feels like the loudest sound in the entire universe and the time it
takes to fully boot it up feels like an eternity.

Example)
Kim: Ugh! My oppa's live performance will be on YouTube past my bed
time…
Hyeri: You should *mol com* tonight.

Kim: Last time I was caught and got grounded.

몰라 Mola
(mol-la)

Phrase. "I Don't Know"
Can be used to avoid answering certain questions that can cause embarrassment.

Example)
Uhyuk: How much do you weigh?
Mina: *Mola!* How can you ask a lady that kind of question?

몸짱 Momzzang / Momjjang
(mom-tchang)

Noun. "Person With Killer Body"
Someone with an awesome body, usually muscular for males and a slim, well-toned body for females.

Example)
Man, I am so fat and my personal trainer told me that it will take full 2 years to transform me into a *momzzang*.

무플 Moo Peul
(mu-p'ŭl)

Noun. "No Comments Received (for something you posted on the Internet)"
This happens when people think your post is not worth commenting on, or it is so controversial that no one dares to get involved.

Example)
Minho: Do you know what is worse than ak peul?
Donny: What is it?
Minho: *Moo peul.* It makes you feel like a nobody.

무대 Moodae
(mu-dae)

Noun. "Stage"
The stage on which KPOP singers perform.

Example)
Centurion looked like a little boy when he was on a TV show, but when he is on *moodae* singing, he is such a sexy man.

모태 솔로 Motae Solo
(mo-tae-sol-lo)

Noun. "Forever Alone"
A compound word made up of "모태" *motae* ("within the womb") and solo. It is used to refer to someone who has never dated anyone and has been single for their entire life.

Example)
As a *motae solo*, Junhee had no idea what kissing feels like, so she devised up a brilliant plan - to fake her drowning and get a mouth-to-mouth.

MR

Noun. "Backgorund Music"
An acronym for "music recorded". It refers to the music portion of a song. MR-removed means leaving only the vocal part of the song, which is a nightmare for some, as it is the ultimate tool to gauge someone's true vocal skills.

Example)
Haha, did you hear the MR version of Kori's song? She really can't carry a tune in a bucket.

문자 Munja
(mun-ja)

Noun. **"Text"**
Most popular means of communication in Korea, especially among the younger generation thanks to the wide propagation of smartphones.

Example)
Munja has completely replaced talking on the phone as the most used means of communication.

Music Bank

Noun. **"Weekly Live Music Show by KBS"**
A weekly live music show by KBS (Korea Broadcasting System) where a winner is announced using a combination of various factors such as the digital music charts, album sales, the number of times the song is played on TV/Radio, and viewers' choice charts.

Example)
I look forward to watching *Music bank* this week because my favorite Oppa's are performing live!

MV

Noun. **"Music Video"**
Each music video has a different "theme" according to the "concept" of the song. In the KPOP industry, a great portion of the production money goes into the making of high-quality music videos.

Example)
8Players' new *MV* has over 3 million views now on YouTube.

뭥미? Mwong Mi?
(mwŏng-mi?)

A slang for "What the…?" It is mostly used among the teens and netizens on the Internet.

Example)
Suzy texted me saying *mwong mi?* I didn't know what the hell she was referring to so I text her back saying *mwong mi?*

마이 스타일 My Style

Phrase. "My Type"
Your ideal type of person.

Example)
Nira: Oh! Oh! Johnny is so *my style*!
Alexa: I hope he feels the same way.

네/아니요 Nae / Aniyo
(ne/a-ni-yo)

Noun. "Yes/No (formal)"
Formal way of saying yes and no. Nae can also be used to acknowledge someone calling you or talking to you.

Example)
Teacher: Vicky! Can you solve this problem?
Vicky: *Nae?* You are talking to me? *Aniyo*, I am afraid I can't…

내게로 와 Nae Ge Ro Wa
(nae-ge-ro wa)

Phrase. "Come to Me"
Asking someone to be either 1) physically or 2) emotionally close to

the speaker. If the latter, it means "come into my heart" and implies the speaker's intention to capture the heart of the listener. It is, therefore, a powerful yet cruel spell one can cast on someone who's already almost enchanted.

Example)
Husband: Honey, *nae ge ro wa <3*
Wife: Ok baby <3
Husband: Oh, can you grab the remote on your way?
Wife: You bastard...

내일 Naeil
(nae-il)

Noun. "Tomorrow"
This is the imaginary place where all the empty promises are piled up.

Example)
Eric: Hey Bryan, when will you clean up the room?
Bryan: I dunno... *naeil?*

냉무 Naeng Moo
(naeng-mu)

Phrase. "End of Message"
An abbreviation for "내용" *nae yong* ("content") "무" *moo* ("nothing"). Its English counterpart is EOM (end of message) used in the subject line of a post or email to indicate to the reader that there is no more content to expect.

Example)
No example here. *Naeng moo!*

낚시 Nak Si
(nak-shi)

Noun. `"Fooling Someone"`
Literal meaning is "fishing", originated from the English word "phishing".
It is used to describe deception/trickery used to achieve a desired outcome
(e.g., scamming). It is also associated with the word "fishing", because the
person who falls prey resembles a hooked fish. This is something to look
out for on April Fool's Day.

Example)
Judy: Jack, if you do me a favor, I will give you kisses!
Jack: Don't *nak si* me girl, I know you will give me a kisses chocolate!

남친/여친 Nam Chin/Yeo Chin
(nam-ch'in/yŏ-ch'in)

Noun. `"Boyfriend/Girlfriend"`
Abbreviation for "남자" *namja* ("man/male") 친구*chingoo* ("friend") and "
여자" *yeoja* ("woman/female") 친구*chingoo* ("friend"). To some,
they are imaginary creatures like a unicorn, which do not exist in the real
world.

Example)
Nora: I have many a lot of guy friends, but no *nam chin*... I wonder why?
Jenna: Maybe because you have so many guy friends, people automatically
assume that you have one?

남대문 Nam Dae Moon
(nam-dae-mun)

Noun. `"XYZ (Examine Your Zipper)"`
Literally means "South Grand Gate", which refers to one of the four grand
gates located around the city of Seoul, but due to the fact that the word
남 (nam) also means "Male", it is figuratively used to refer to the "Men's
Grand Gate" = the front zipper of a (man's) pants.

Example)
Keira: Your *nam dae moon*!
Jim: Hm? You want to go to the South Grand Gate?
Keria: No! Your zipper is open!

남사/여사 친구 Namsa/Yeosa Chingoo
(n nam-sa/yŏ-sa ch'in-'gu)

Noun. "A Male/Female Friend"
While "남자 친구*namja chingoo*" and "여자 친구*yeoja chingoo*" mean
boyfriend/girlfriend, "남사*namsa*" and "여사*yeosa*" are short for "남자
namja ("male) *saram* ("human") and "여자" *yeoja* ("female") 사람*saram*
("human")". Hence, it is used to make clear that the person being referred to
is just a friend that happens to be of that gender.

Example)
Monica: Hey, you two make a cute couple!
Tom: No, no, no – She is just a *yeosa chingoo*!
Jennifer: Exactly! He is not my type. He is a *namsa chingoo*!

네이버 Naver

Noun. "Korea's Almighty Internet Portal (Google + Yahoo)"
Korea's largest Internet portal site. It provides a myriad of services such
as web search, shopping, blogs, news, music, directions, and so on. Its
presence is so significant that ranking on Naver's real-time search results is
what many KPOP idols dream of.

Example)
Abe: Bro, can you Google this for me?
Nielson: Forget Google. Everybody *Navers* in Korea, mate!

넘사벽 Neom Sa Byeok
(nŏm-sa-byŏk)

Noun. "Something Unbeatable/Unbelievable"
An abbreviation for "넘을 수 없는*neom eul soo eop neun* ("unclimbable")
사차원의*sacha won eui* ("fourth-dimensional") 벽 *byeok* ("wall")". It

is used to describe someone or something that is beyond one's control (unbeatable) or comprehension (unbelievable), and it can be used both as a compliment and a ridicule.

Example)
Doyle: So I had 3 shots of Vodka, 1 bottle of Soju, and 2 glasses of wine and I'm still sober?
Mina: When it comes to drinking, you are *neom sa byeok*.

Netizen

Noun. "Internet User"
A compound word made up of "Internet" and "citizen". They are notorious for their mob mentality where they leave an endless amount of negative comments on news articles, sometimes causing an end to one's career or even leading to a suicide.

Example)
Hong Sung's got arrested for stealing at the supermarket. I can't wait to see all the harsh comments the *Netizens* have come up with.

뉴페 New Pe
(nyu-p'e)

Noun. "New Member"
Its literal meaning is "New Face" 뉴*new*페이스 *pe i seu* (face – no F sound in Korean). While it is similar to "Newbie", it doesn't necessarily mean someone inexperienced. It refers to someone who joins a group for the first time, regardless of their experience.

Example)
Ning: Boring! Aren't we getting any *new pe*'s to our band this semester?
Jenna: I got a major overhaul through plastic surgery. Does that count as a *new pe*?

뇌섹남 New Saek Nam
(noe-sek-nam)

Noun. "Man with a Sexy Brain"

An abbreviation for "뇌가" *noe ga* ("brain is") "섹시한" *sek si han* ("sexy") "남자" *nam ja* ("male"). It is used to describe a man who is smart and witty, making him "sexy" on the inside. Hence, someone whose does not look particularly attractive can still earn this title.

Example)
Sohyang: You know that new guy in our math class, right? I heard he got a perfect score on SAT!
Gloria: Wow – I didn't know that she was such a *noe saek nam*!

뉴비 Newbie

Noun. "Someone Who is Inexprienced in a Particular Field/ Activity"

If a new KPOP idol has just debuted, he/she is a newbie in the music industry and has a lot of sunbae's to show respect to.

Example)
Jun: Hi guys, I am a former professional baseball player!
Taro: Welcome! But yoga is a completely different from baseball You are a *newbie* yogi!

NG

Noun. "No Good"

An abbreviation for "No Good". It is what the director/producer says during a filming of a movie or a show when an actor makes a mistake (e.g., forgetting their line or bursting into laughter). The portion is discarded and the scene is filmed again until a good take is achieved.

Example)
NG! You were not supposed to close your eyes when you kiss her!

노안 Noan
(no-an)

Noun. "Face That Looks Older Than Actual Age"
The exact opposite of 동안 *dong an.*

Example)
Andy is only 22 but he has the face of a 40-year-old man. What's more amazing is, his whole family looks older than their actual age. I guess they all have *noan* DNA running in their blood.

녹화방송 Nok Hwa Bang Song
(no-k'wa-bang-song)

Noun. "Airing of a Pre-recorded (Show)"
A compound word made up of "녹화" *nok hwa* ("recording") + "방송" *bang song* ("airing, broadcast"). This is the format used by most TV shows, that have a script to follow, and in which NGs need to be re-done.

Example)
Yoshi: I wonder how they keep a straight face when making such funny jokes?
Ina: Because it's a *nok hwa bang song*! I bet they had lots of NG's.

놀토 Nol To
(nol-to)

Noun. "Saturday-Off"
Literal meaning is "playing Saturday". The term came into existence in 2012 when public schools in Korea adopted a five-day school system, making Saturday an off day for students.

Example)
Kimberly: Just 10 seconds left…
Mary: Huh?
Kimberly: Yay! It's *nol to*!
Mary: You didn't have to wake me up for that…

눈치 Noon Chi
(nun-ch'i)

Noun. "Tact", "Common Sense"
An essential social skill which is a combination of various elements such as being able to quickly read others' emotions and make necessary adjustments accordingly. Those who can't are considered a potential threat due to their unpredictability (e.g., talking about someone's ex at their wedding).

Example)
Uchi was a cosseted only child who got everything he wanted growing up, and for that he was know for his lack of *noon chi*.

누나 Noona
(nu-na)

Noun. "Older Sister"
A term used exclusively by a younger male to an older female, but it can't be used to a stranger unless permission is given or until enough emotional intimacy has been established. It can, however, be used by a younger male to address an older female in a relationship.

Example)
Noona! Where is mom?

누나 로맨스 Noona Romance

Noun. "Older Woman Falling in Love With a Younger Guy"
In K-Dramas, it often starts with a strong denial but eventually ends as the female character gives in and accepts the reality.

Example)
What? There is no way I'm having *noona romance* with him! He is way younger than me and I like him only as a dong saeng. Hm, on a second thought, he is kinda cute.

누나킬러 Noona Killer

Noun. "Hot Young Male Capable of Making Noona's Fall in Love With Him"

A hot young male who is capable of making noonas fall in love with him, using various tactics such as aegyo and eye smiles.

Example)
Andrew is so popular among noona's because of his cuteness. He is such a *noona killer.*

노래 Norae
(no-rae)

Noun. "Song"
A song and the act of singing.

Example)
Norae and choom are the 2 most sought after talents in idol groups.

노래방 Noraebang
(no-rae-bang)

Noun. "Karaoke"
A place where many people go for 2-cha or 3-cha (2nd round or 3rd round of drinking and partying). People go there to let their hair down and bring out their "party animal" side. Usually the final destination for a company group dinner.

Example)
Ya! Let's go to *Noraebang*! I am so drunk and I have to sing my favorite song!

누구 Nugu
(nu-gu)

Phrase. "Who"

Used to ask about someone you don't know, but it is also used to look down on a person whom you want to make look small.

Example)
Bobae: Hey, it's me!
Chorin: *Nugu?*

오글 O Geul
(o-gŭl)

Phrase. "Cringing"

Literal meaning is "(fingers/toes) curling", which describes your body's natural response to something stimulating, both positive and negative (e.g., fear, shame, joy, and etc.). In Korean, however, this is exclusively used to describe a situation that makes you feel embarrassed, hence, it is an expression of aversion.

Example)
Mini: That new boy in our science class is such a dork. He proposed to his girlfriend during a gym class and got rejected.
Arthur: That is so *o geul o geul…* I feel embarrassed.

오징어 O Jing Eoh
(o-jing-ŏ)

Noun. "Ugly Face"

Literally meaning "squid", but recently it has been used to refer to someone hideous, after a hilarious anecdote circulated on the Internet. The story goes like this: a couple went to a movie starring Won Bin, who is one of the best looking actors in Korea. While watching the movie, the woman thought he wasn't so good looking. After the movie, however, she turned and looked at her boyfriend, and all of a sudden there was a "squid" sitting next to her.

Example)

People avoided being in the same picture with Marco, because his overwhelming visual always made them look like an *oh jing eoh.*

오바이트 Oba Iteu
(o-ba-i-t'ŭ)

Noun. "To Throw Up"
Konglish for "over eat", but it is used to refer to the general act of vomiting.

Example)
Miso: Oh crap! I jus *oba iteu*!
Christina: Oh no! Did you drink bad milk or something?
Miso: No, I accidentally saw a picture your bare face.

오지랖 Oh Ji Rap
(o-ji-rap)

Noun. "Being Nosy"
Being overly curious and meddlesome, such as gossiping and prying into each other's affairs.

Example)

Umi: Hey! You should be a rapper!
Joe: Rapper? What rapper?
Umi: The *Oh Ji Rap*per! Cause you have a finger in every pie.

OME (Oh My Eyes)

Phrase. "Something You Want to Avoid Seeing"
An abbreviation for oh my eyes!". Something horrendous which you hope that you don't have to see with your own eyes.

Example)
Tae: Oh, don't come in! I'm in my birthday suit!
Wonhee: Birthday suit What does that mean?

Tae: It means I am butt naked!
Wonhee: Oh! *OME*! *OME*!

어제 Oje (Eoje)
(ŏ-je)

Noun. "Yesterday"
The place where your regrets are piled up.

Example)
Oje, you said tomorrow! And you still haven't finished your homework?

올드미스 Old Miss

Noun. "Woman Who is Old and Not Married"
Indirect/less offensive way of saying "spinster". Keep in mind that this
is different from "돌싱" dol sing, because it refers to someone who has
become single through a recent divorce.

Example)
Ju Ju: Hey, why is your aunt so cranky today?
Sena: I dunno… maybe she's having her *old miss* hysteria!

어머 Omo (Eo meo)!
(ŏ-mŏ)

Interjection. "Oh My!"
Spontaneous response that comes out in amazing, embarrassing, surprising,
and scary moments. It is only used by females, and if used by a male he
could be suspected as gay.

Example)
Yun: Did you hear that? Carla farted on the show.
Michelle: *Omo!* That is so hilarious.

오나전 Ona Jeon
(o-na-jŏn)

Adjective. "Completely"
A typo of "완전" wan jeon ("completely"), which has been widely used among the younger generation because it sounds fun, but it is also used in real life conversations as well.

Example)
Joann: Waaaaa.... I am *ona jeon* in trouble …
Doug: What happened?
Joann: My boss found out that I went out the day I called in sick…

오늘 Onul (Oneul)
(o-nŭl)

Noun. "Today"
The day you referred to yesterday when you said that you would do things "tomorrow".

Example)
Onul, I am really going to pop the question. I hope she says yes.

오빠 Oppa
(o-ppa)

Noun. "Older Brother"
A term used by a younger female to address an older male. It can be used between siblings or anybody who has enough emotional intimacy with the recipient. Guys are known to love hearing this from their dong saeng girls as it gives them a sense of superiority and dominance. Many girls use this to their advantage, by calling someone oppa and asking for favors because it generally yields a higher success rate.

Example)
Daisy: Sam, can you do the dishes for me?
Sam: Hell naw.

Daisy: *Oppa~! Pweeeeease~! (Baby voice)*
Sam: Oh, ok.

오크 Ork
(o-k'ŭ)

Noun. "Ugly Woman"
The name of a savage, warlike, hideous monster race that appears in fantasy stories. Because of their gigantic body and ugly appearance, it is often used to disparage females who are unattractive.

Example)
Tommy: Ugh! Look at that *Ork*! Let's beat it up!
Shawn: Dude, chillax! That' is your sister!
Tommy: OMG… I must have been playing Warcraft too much…

OST

Noun. "Original Sound Track"
A track specifically composed and sung for a soap opera (drama) or a movie. It is usually played as a background music during important scenes, such as when romance suddenly develops (e.g., kissing) or at the end of the show with the credit roll.

Example)
These days, *OST*'s are sung by many famous singers.

OTL

Chat Acronym. "Frustrated", "Discouraged"
Emoticon that symbolizes a man kneeling down with both hands on the ground, where O is the head, T is the arms , and L is the legs. It is a simple yet powerful way to convey complex emotions.

Example)
Soo: Why the long face?
Minho: I drunk-dialed my ex last night *OTL*.

어떡해 Otoke
(ŏ-ttŏ-k'ae)

Interjection. **"Oh No!"**
Can be translated as "What should I do?". Also used to express amazement, embarrassment, and confusion.

Example)
I forgot to do my homework! *Otoke!*
Jenny: Hey, I got 2 tickets to the Dram Concert~!
Michael: What? *Otoke?*

OTP

Noun. **"One True Pairing"**
Your most favored and preferred parings of people within a group.
Describes two people who especially get along really well with each other, regardless of romance involved.

Example)
Jenny and Tony are *OTP* – they are like brother and sister but they are also like boyfriend and girlfriend.

아웃오브안중 Out of An Joong
(a-u-do-bŭ-an-jung)

Phrase. **"Out of Consideration"**
"안중" *an joong* literally means "in the eyes" so if someone or something is out of "안중", or "out of sight", someone or something is of no importance.

Example)
Yurim: I lost so much weight and I feel awesome! I think I look so beautiful! I don't have to beg him for attention anymore. I can get someone better than him.
Phillip: Whoa, girl! He is so *out of an joong* now!

P방 P Bang

Noun.
Kids' and teenagers' way of saying "PC Bang", the place where all the liberated souls (read: students) gather to indulge in their freedom. Their freedom ends at10PM, the time when the "shut down" rule become effective.

Example)
Tony: Yay! Schools over! Let's go to our sacred haven!
Zack: Huh? What do you mean?
Tony: *P bang*, my friend, *P bang…*

팔불출 Pal Bool Chool
(p'al-bul-ch'ul)

Noun. "Someone Who Habitually Brags About Their Significant Other"
Literally someone who was born one month prematurely, but it has been figuratively used to describe someone who is dull. In real life, it also refers to a married man who keeps bragging about his wife all the time.

Example)
Beginning this year, no *pal bool chool*s are allowed at the high school's reunion because there are still people who are not married.

PD

Noun. "Program Director" "Producer"
The person who is in charge of the making of a TV show/program.

Example)
If you want to earn a spot in that variety TV show, you really have to suck up to Kim *PD*.

Pedo Noona

Noun. "Older Female with an Interest in Younge Male Idols"
A compound word made up of "pedophile" and "noona". It refers to an older female with an interest in a younger male idol in an inappropriate and even sexual way.

Example)
Be careful, Patricia is an infamous *pedo noona!* I heard her boyfriend just graduated from high school.

빼빼로 데이 Pepero Day
(ppe-ppe-ro de-i)

Noun. "Valentine's Day in November (11/11)"
November 11th, the day when people exchange Peperos (chocolate-covered long biscuit sticks) because the numbers look like four sticks (11/11). Similar to Valentine's Day, but many think it is just another marketing gimmick (and an insult to all singles).

Example)
To celebrate *Pepero Day*, Wendy bought 5 packs of Pepero and finished them in one sitting.

피켓팅 Picketing

Noun. "Blood Splattering/Splashing Ticket Sale"
A term used to describe how difficult and even brutal it is for KPOP fans to get a ticket to a TV music show in Korea. Its intensity is, therefore, likened to that of a battlefield.

Example)
Jenny got hospitalized as a result of the *picketing war* she participated. The blood-covered ticket is the Medal of Honor to her.

핑프 Ping Peu
(p'ing-p'ŭ)

Noun. "Finger Princess"
Short for "pinger (no F sound in Korean) princess". It refers to someone who sits on their ass in front of a computer all day long and orders people around by sending chat messages.

Example)
Brother: Hm? Got a message from sis…
Sis: Hey, can you get me a cup of coffee?
Brother: What the… Hey! Don't be a *ping peu* and get your own coffee!

Plastic Prince

Noun. "Good Looking Male Who Achieved a Flower Boy Status Through Plastic Surgery"
A good looking gorgeous male who achieved the "flower boy" status through plastic surgery.

Example)
Tony came back to the showbiz after his 2-year break. During that time he went through a massive transformation incorporating plastic surgery. He looks really beautiful, but he can't deny the fact that he is a *plastic prince!*

Plastic Surgery

Noun. "Surgically Altering One's Physical Appearance"
The practice of surgically altering one's physical appearance. Double eyelids, fuller forehead, reshaping chin, and getting a nose job are among the most popular.

Example)
Mom, dad, today I decided to become a changed person… through *plastic surgery!*

포샵 Po Shop
(p'o-syap)

Noun. "Photoshop"

The omnipotent computer graphics/image editing software that turns ugly into pretty, and skinny and fatty into super models.

Example)
Alexis: Summer is just around the corner!
Minjoo: We need to hit the gym and get in shape!
Alexis: Girl, no need to do that.
Minjoo: Why?
Alexis: I just learned how to use *Po Shop*!

포장마차 Pojangmacha
(p'o-jang-ma-ch'a)

Noun. "Outdoor Korean Street Food Pub"

An outdoor Korean street food pub. A small tented spot that is either on wheels or is a street stall. It sells a variety of popular street foods such as tteokbokki, mandu, and anju (bar snacks). In K-Dramas, this is a place where people go to in order to drown their sadness or anger in bottles of soju. Other clichéd settings include subordinates confronting their boss about something or one making "drunk love confessions (asking out)" to a secret admirer (with the help of alcohol!).

Example)
After work, Dohwan and Yonggi got together and headed straight to *Pojangmacha* where they emptied 8 bottles of Soju.

품절남/녀 Poom Jeol Nam/Nyeo
(p'um-jŏl-lam/nyŏ)

Noun. "Married Man/Woman"

A compound word made up of "품절" *poom jeol* ("sold out") + "남/녀" nam/nyeo ("man/woman"). Someone who just became an unavailable player/participant in the dating market.

Example)
Juan: What… Hector and Susana are getting married?
Victor: Yup, they are a *poom jeol nam/nyeo* couple.

PR

Noun. "Picture Request"
A term used on fan sites by when users request pictures of an idol or a specific event.

Example)

Toya: Got some pics at the concert last night!
Cecilia: *PR*! Can you send them to my Ka Tok?

Prince of Asia

Noun. "Lee Kwang Soo"
A nickname originally given to the actor and singer Jang Geun Suk for his overwhelming popularity in Asia (especially in Japan). Recently, however, Lee Kwang Soo has taken over the title, thanks to a successful TV show "Running Man" that is incredibly popular in Asia (especially in China and Hong Kong)

Example)
When I went to Hong Kong, so many people surrounded me asking for my signature. It must be because I look like Lee Kwang Soo! Now I kinda know what living as the *Prince of Asia* would feel like.

Q_Q

Noun. "Crying"
An emoticon used to symbolize crying.

Example)
After watching the new K-melodrama, I was literally *Q_Q*.

레알 Rae Al
(rae-al)

Interjection. "For Real"

An English word pronounced in a Spanish-style, as the Spanish football team Real Madrid is hugely popular in Korea. It can also be used to express surprise or to assert that something is genuine or is true.

Example)
Mario: I aced the math test!
Yasiel: *Rae al?*
Mario: Yeah, dude, for real!

Rainism

Noun. "Anything That is Influenced or Touched by Rain (Bi)"

The title of the song by Korean singer Bi (Rain). It is used to describe anything that is influenced or touched by him, or the act of someone trying to imitate him.

Example)
Jeong put on a black leather jacket and dark sun glasses and started doing the Rain dance. He sure has serious *Rainism* going on.

Red Sun

Interjection. "Hypnosis"

Popularized by a Korean hypnotist who says this to his client while inducing hypnosis. For this reason, when someone says this, they pretend they are hypnotized (just for fun).

Example)
Hey man, you talk too much! Let me put you to sleep. *Red Sun!*

Repackaged Album

Noun. "Full Album that is Re-released with a New Title Track"
A full album that is re-released with the addition of a new title track, along with other bonus tracks and remixes.

Example)
Because of the disagreements over the contract, New Boys couldn't release a new album. Instead, the company put a *repackaged album* on the market.

Rookie

Noun. "Newbie"
An actor, idol, or group who recently made a debut in the entertainment industry, regardless of age.

Example)
Wonki is an old *rookie* who made his debut at age 35.

S Line

Noun. "Curvaceous Female Body"
A curvaceous female body. When standing sideways, the shape of the body with a flat stomach and curvy backside resembles the Latin letter "S".

Example)
The first thing I need to get the *S Line* is to cut down on the sweets.

S.K.

Noun. "South Korea"
The birthplace of KPOP, K-Drama, Hallyu (Korean Wave), Kimchi, Bibimbap, Bulgogi, Aegyo, etc. For many foreigners who know South Korea only through the media, it is viewed as a country where war is imminent (vs. North Korea), everybody drinks two bottles of soju every day, sings like a pro at Karaoke, and has a black belt in Taekwondo.

Example)
Lokkin: I'm going to *S.K.* for a summer vacay!
Juan: Where?
Lokkin: *S.K.,* South Korea, yo!

사바사 Sa Ba Sa
(sa-ba-sa)

Abbreviation. "Differ From Individual to Individual"
An abbreviation for "사람" *saram* ("person") by사람*saram*. This is similar to "Case By Case", and its closest English equivalent is "YMMV (Your Mileage May Vary)".

Example)
Molly: How is the new Korean restaurant in K-Town?
Kwon: Well, sometimes good, sometimes so-so.
Molly: Why?
Kwon: I guess it's *sa ba sa* – some days there is a good chef on duty but other days there must be horrible chef on duty.

사이다 Sa I Da
(sa-i-da)

Noun. Adjective. "Hits the Spot"
Opposite of "고구마" go gu ma ("a stuffy/suffocating situation or someone who is insensitive or slow-witted"). It originated from the word "cider", a carbonated Korean soda similar to Sprite or 7UP, because drinking it makes you feel refreshed. It is a powerful antidote for "고구마".

Example)
Mindy: *Sa i da...* I need *Sa i da*!
Hoon: What's wrong?
Mindy: The male character hasn't confessed his love to the female character in the past 6 episodes and it's driving me crazy!

사랑해 Sa Rang Hae
(sa-rang-hae)

Phrase. `"I Love You"`
It is probably the most spoken (abused) phrase throughout KPOP songs and K-Dramas.

Example)
No, I don't hate you. *Sa Rang Hae!*

생방송 Saeng Bang Song
(saeng-bang-song)

Noun. `"Live Airing"`
A compound word made up of "생" *saeng* ("live/alive") + "방송" *bang song* ("airing, broadcast"). It is a format used by major weekly music shows (e.g., Music Bank). Because everything is performed live, mistakes made on the stage will be broadcast unedited. This is something many "vocally weak" idols are afraid of, but it is a great opportunity for those with superior "vocals" to show off their talents.

Example)
Yeonhee: I feel anxious from watching Music Bank…!
Tim: Why?
Yeonhee: Because it's *saeng bang song*… I worry about my oppa's making a mistake on the stage!

생얼 Saeng Eol
(saeng-ŏl)

Noun. `"Face Without Any Make-up on"`
생 saeng means "bare", and 얼 eol is an abbreviation for 얼굴 *eol gool*, "face", hence "bare face". To some girls, this is their worst nightmare.

Example)
Mark: If I were a cop, I would arrest you!
Jennifer: Awww, so you can keep me in your jail?

Mark: No, for having a weapon of mass destruction.
Jennifer: What weapon?
Mark: Your *saeng eol.*

생파 Saeng Pa
(saeng-p'a)

Noun. "Birthday Party"
An abbreviation for "생일" *saeng il* ("birthday") "파티" (party).

Example)
Mary: Tomorrow's my birthday!
Jin: Where the *saeng pa* at?

생선 Saeng Seon
(saeng-sŏn)

Noun. "Birthday Gift"
Acronym for "생일" *saeng il* ("birthday") "선물" *seon mool* ("gift"). It is widely used by the teens because it sounds funny (because it also means "fish").

Example)
Hanna: I hope you brought *saeng seon* for my birthday.
Min: Huh? Fish?
Hanna: No! Birthday gift!

쌩유 Saeng You
(ssaeng-yu)

Phrase. "Thank You"
A funny variation of saying "thank you", which was first used by a comedian, Yoo Jae Seok. Instead of pronouncing the "th" sound, you substitute it with a strong S sound.

Example)

After 10 years of living in Korea, Brandon, a native New Yorker, started feeling confused over which to say. "Thank You" or "*Saeng You*"?

사극 Sageuk
(sa-gŭk)

Noun. "Historical Korean Drama"
A historical Korean drama set in a period earlier than modern day Korea (the 1900's).

Example)
Charlie will be acting as a 13th-century blade smith in an upcoming *sageuk*.

삭발 Sak Bal
(sak-bal)

Noun. "Shaving One's Head"
Something male idols have to go through before joining the army for their military obligation. It is an emotional moment because cutting one's hair means disconnection from the outside world.

Example)
Victoria couldn't stop crying as she watched her oppa, Chanyong, was getting a *sak bal* because it meant a 2-year-long farewell.

삼촌팬 Samchon Fans
(sam-ch'on-p'aen)

Noun. "Uncle Fans"
It refers to the fan demographic (aged 30-40) who follow girl group idols. They are known for their ability to spend more on jo gong because most of them have a full-time job.

Example)
Thanks to their overwhelming cuteness, Hello Ladies have tens of

thousands *samchon fans* over the age of 40.

상남자 Sangnamja
(sang-nam-ja)

Noun. "Real Man"
A man who possesses the stereotypical male characteristics such as physical strength, mental toughness, and paternal (fatherly) instincts, in contrast to "flower boys".

Example)
Mason drank 2 bottles of Soju in one sitting in order to make him look like a *sangnamja*, but he only became an alcoholic.

사생 Saseng
(sa-saeng)

Noun. "Overly Obsessive Fan"
The overly obsessive fans who engage in outrageous and even dangerous behavior towards their idols, including stalking them and breaking into their homes. They are compared to stalkers and peeping toms.

Example)
Did you hear? Marcus broke into HIHI's home and stole their photo album! That's a serious crime and something only a *saseng* would do.

세젤예 Se Jel Ye
(se-jel-ye)

Noun. "The Most Beautiful in the World"
An abbreviation for "세상에서" *se sang e seo* ("in the world") "제일" *je il* ("number one") "예쁜" *ye bbeun* ("beautfiul").

Example)
Evil Queen: Mirror, mirror, on the wall, who is the prettiest of all?
Mirror: You. You are the *se jel ye*.
Evil Queen: You are promoted to Deluxe Mirror.

셀카 Selca

Noun. "Selfie"

An abbreviation for "self camera". It is the act of holding one's camera and taking a shot of oneself. With a little touch-up using a photo editing app, you can become an "얼짱" ulzzang ("best face").

Example)
Heemin takes one too many *selca's*. Her Instagram is full of photos of her faces.

선수 Seon Soo
(sŏn-su)

Phrase. "Player"

Literally meaning "someone who is highly skilled at something", such as an athlete, but it is also used to refer to a "player" who flirts and is good at seducing someone.

Example)
Youngmi: Be careful with Jinho! He's such a *seon soo*!
Yena: I like atheletes! What does he play?
Youngmi: No! It means he's a player!

스샷 Seu Shot
(sŭ-syat)

Noun. "Screen Capture"

An abbreviation for "스크린" screen "샷" shot. It is the act of capturing the displayed image on a device's monitor (e.g., computer, smartphone, and etc.).

Example)
George: I got a message from my crush!
Winnie: I don't believe you. Send me a *seu shot*!

샤방 Sha Bang
(sya-bang)

Adjective. "Bling Bling", "Dazzling"
A term used to describe someone's radiating beauty. A cliched example: a girl tosses her hair in slow-mo, with some sort of celestial lights and glittering CG surround her, making everyone's jaws drop in amazement.

Example)
Joon: Wow! Why are you so *sha bang sha bang* today?
Bonnie: I have a date today, so I spent some time preening myself.

식신 Shik Shin
(shik-shin)

Noun. "Food Hogger"
A compound word made up of two Chinese words: "식" *shik* ("to eat") "신" *shin* ("god" or "demon"). It refers to someone who shows exceptional abilitiy to devour a massive amount of food at a super-human speed. Jeong Joon Ha of the Infinity Challenge was a famous "식신".

Example)
Wanso only weighs 100 pounds but she is a formidable *shik shin*. She eats 5,000 calories a day.

심쿵 Shim Koong
(shim-k'ung)

Noun. Interjection. "Heart Racing"
An abbreviation for "심장이" *shim jang* ("heart") "쿵쾅" *koong kwang* ("sound of the heart beating/racing") = "Heart is Racing/Beating Rapidly". This is a spontaneous reaction by your central nerve system that occurs upon seeing your bias.

Example)
Nero: Oh, wow! We almost got ran over by a car!
Nick: *Shim koong…*

신곡 Shin Gok
(shin-'gok)

Noun. `"New Song"`
A compound word made up of two Chinese words: 신 *shin* ("new") 곡 *gok* ("song"). It is the subject of extreme anticipation by fanboys/girls because it means their idols are coming back from a hiatus.

Example)
Fans all over the world have been waiting for UIUI's *shin gok*, which incorporates the elements of jazz and funk.

신의아들 Shine Adeul
(shi-nǔi-a-dǔl)

Noun. `"Someone Who is Exempt from Mandatory Miltary Service"`
"신의" *shine* means "God's" and "아들" *adeul* means "son", so its literal meaning is "son of God". It is used to refer to someone who is exempt from Korea's mandatory military service, especially with no apparent reason but through various means not available to the general public. This "privilege" is often abused by the rich and the powerful (i.e., a member of the National Assembly, Chaebols, and so on) which causes many social problems.

Example)
Dana: So, why did he not go to the army?
Russ: News says he was diagnosed with "happy virus"
Dana: That's B.S.! There is no such thing, right?
Russ: I guess he's just a *shine adeul*.

쇼케이스 Showcase

Noun. `"Public Performance"`
A term that can be used as a noun or a verb, it refers to singers performing in public, in order to "show off" their skills.

Example)
At this audition, Wacko *showcased* his crazy breakdance skills.

셧다운 Shut Down

Also known as the "Cinderella Law", it is a regulation that went into effect back in 2011. It prohibits children of age 16 and under from playing online games between the hours of 12:00 A.M. and 6:00 A.M.

Example)
Kid 1: Who's our biggest enemy?
Kid 2: Teachers? Parents?
Kid 1: No! It's the *shut down* rule!

싸인회 Sign Hwae
(ssa-in-hoe)

Noun. "Signing Event"
A dream come true moment for KPOP fanboys/girls because it is a rare opportunity to meet their bias in person, and they are welcome to bring their belongings for the bias to autograph.

Example)
The *sign hwae* by Jamie J attracted more than 10,000 people, because everybody wanted to see him in person.

신상 Shin Sang
(sin-sang)

Noun. "New Product"
This burns a hole in a KPOP fan boy/girl's pocket. It is especially detrimental to those with an impulse disorder, or someone who wants to earn the title of "early adopter" or "trend leader".

Example)
Girlfriend: Hey baby, let's go to the mall and have lunch?
Boyfriend: Lunch? You mean you want to buy that *sin sang* dress right?
Girlfriend: Just give me your card!

Skinship

Noun. "Physical Contact"
A Konglish for "physical contact", such as holding hands, hugging, and etc. "manner hands (hovering hands)" is the act of trying to avoid any unnecessary "skinship".

Example)
My boyfriend likes *skinship* too much! We've only dated once!

슬로건 Slogan

Noun. "Banner With the Group or a Member's Name"
A thin towel, or a banner, with the name of a group or an idol printed on it. They are made and sold by the company the idols belong to, or they are made by fans and distributed for free at concerts to show their "support" during a performance.

Example)
At the peak of the concert, all the fans took out their *slogans*.

Small Face

Noun. "Face That is Small in Size (a compliment)"
A face that is small in size. It is a compliment as it is believed that smaller faces make facial features look well-defined and thus photogenic while giving a youthful look.

Example)
Hyoju has such a *small face!* She should audition to become an actor. She'd look great on TV.

SNS

Noun. "Social Media"
An abbreviation for "Social Networking Service", It is a term not widely used outside of Korea. When used in news articles, it refers to celebrities'

Facebook, Twitter, Weibo, Instagram etc. accounts.

Example)
After the scandal broke out, Hunter K shut down all of his *SNS* accounts.

소주 Soju
(so-ju)

Noun. "Traditional Korean Alcoholic Drink"

A traditional Korean alcoholic drink made by distilling starchy grains such as rice, sweet potatoes, potatoes, or tapioca. It is the most popular drink among Koreans and is an indispensable part of Korean life and K-Dramas. Most of it is packaged in green bottles, and it is one of the top-selling liquors in the world.

Example)
Hey man, long time no see! Let's go pop a few bottles of *Soju!*

속도 위반 Sokdo Wiban
(sok-do wi-ban)

Noun. "Getting Pregnant Before Marriage"

A compound word made up of "속도" *sokdo* ("speed") + "위반" *wi ban* ("violation"). It refers to a couple that is expecting a baby before officially marrying. This was something to be ashamed of in Korea in the past, but as the society became more open and westernized, it became something to be congratulated on. In some K-Drama settings, couples often decide to use pregnancy as leverage to secure "marriage approval" from their parents (similar to a "shotgun wedding").

Example)
Bobby: They just made a wedding announcement!
Windy: Wow, that is a surprise!
Bobby: I'm positive that they had a *sokdo wiban* because of her belly.
Windy: That's called a beer belly, dude.

솔까말 Sol Kka Mal
(sol-kka-mal)

Phrase. TBH ("To Be Honest")
An abbreviation for "솔직히" *sol jik hi* ("honestly") "까놓고" *kka not go* ("openly, publicly") "말해서" *mal hae seo* ("speaking"). It is used more often on the Internet than in real life conversations.

Example)
Mina: *Sol kka mal*, not too many people like oppa as much as I do.
Hailey: I don't think so! Don't underestimate my love for oppa!

썸남/썸녀 Some Nam / Some Nyeo
(ssŏm-nam/ssŏm-nyŏ)

Noun. "Someone You Are Seeing"
Derived from the word "something", it refers to a male or a female who's got "something (romantic)" going on with another. If you are a male, you would have "some nyeo (female)", a girl you have been dating, but you are not officially going out with her yet. Hence you just have "something (romantic)" going on with her.

Example)
No, she is not my girlfriend. She is just one of my many *some nyeo's*.

수능 Soo Neung
(su-nŭng)

Noun. "College Scholastic Ability Test (College Entrance Exam)"
Judgment day for all third-year graduating high school students because it is the single most important factor colleges look at when evaluating applicants. Its significance is enormous, to the point where emergency ambulances and police cars are on standby to transport students who are struggling to make it to the test site on time.

Example)
Soo neung can mean freedom to many, but it can also mean another year of

jail time if they don't pass it.

Spazzing

Noun. "Freaking Out"
Your body's natural reaction when you are surrounded with extremely strong emotions (joy, excitement, etc.). Fan boys/girls experience this when they see their favorite idol in person. It is often accompanied by screaming and in extreme cases, passing out.

Example)
Henry: Why is she *spazzing*?
Woody: Oh, she just received an invitation to her bias' private fan meeting.

스펙 Spec

Noun. "Job Qualifications"
Originally derived from "specification", but its meaning has been changed to refer to "work experience" and other "extracurricular activities". Many young job applicants spend a significant amount of time and money on beefing up their "spec" (e.g., studying abroad for language training), in order to win the cut-throat competition in the job market.

Example)
Martha didn't even bother applying for the job because she thought she doesn't have enough *specs* to compete with other applicants.

스포 Spo

Noun. "Spoiler"
Short for "spoiler", which is the despicable act of revealing a previously unknown aspect of something, thereby completely ruining someone's opportunity to learn and/or enjoy.

Example)
Don't say a word about the last episode! No one wants you to *spo* it again!

싸가지 Ssa Ga Ji
(ssa-ga-ji)

Noun. "Rude/Selfish Person"
Someone whose attitude is extremely inconsiderate towards others, to the point that it causes rage.

Example)
Jenny: Oh! Free money on the ground!
Eric: Dude! That's my money!
Jenny: Finders keepers!
Eric: You *ssa ga ji*…

쌍수 Ssang Soo
(ssang-su)

Noun. "Double-eyelid Surgery"
One of the most widely performed plastic surgeries among Koreans who wish to have their eyes appear bigger and more defined. Due to the simplicity of the procedure, many don't even consider it as "surgery" but a simple "beauty enhancement".

Example)
Ssang soo is considered an "upgrade".

싼티 Ssanti
(ssan-t'i)

Noun. "Looking Tawdry", "Unclassy"
An expression of disparagement, but some idols have incorporated it to make it a part of their unique character.

Example)
OMG, that twerking is so *ssanti*. I wonder if her parents say anything?

썩소 Sseok So
(ssŏk-so)

Noun. `"Awkwawrd Smile not Coming From Genuine Pleasure"`
An abbreviation for "썩은" *sseok eun* ("rotten") "미소" *miso* ("smile"). It is a facial expression occurring from the incongruence between your body and mind, where your mind says "shi*", but your face is trying to smile. It usually ends up as a smile with only one end of the mouth turning upward.

Example)
Mandy: Guessing from your *sseok so*, you are made at me, right?
Jillian: Are you kidding me? You just totaled my car!

Stage

Noun. `"Place on Which Idols Perform"`
When combined with another word such as "come back (stage)", "good bye (stage)", it is used to mean "performance"

Example)
Shine Shine is having a special *stage* for the homeless! They are so warm-hearted!

Stan

Noun. `"Obsessive Fan"`
A compound word made up of "stalker" and "fan". It describes an avid and obsessive fan. While the term carries a negative connotation, it is not as bad as saseng.

Example)
I hired a private detective and found out my Oppa's address… I am afraid that I am becoming a *stan*.

서브 유닛 Sub-unit

Noun. <mark>"Smaller (project) Group Within a Larger Group"</mark>
A group formed to serve a different market segment, and while generally comprising existing members, new members are often added just for the project.

Example)
JOA created a *sub-unit* consisting only rappers.

선배 Sunbae
(sŏn-bae)

Noun. <mark>"Senior in a Certain Field"</mark>
Someone with more experience or seniority in a certain field, regardless of age. As a sunbae, one assumes the leadership and provides care to their hoobae's.

Example)
Sunbae! We will do anything you say! Just give us an order.

서포트 Support
(sŏ-p'o-t'ŭ)

Noun. <mark>"Large Fan-Events to Support Their Biases"</mark>
The large events run by KPOP fans and fan clubs to show their love. Examples include buying meal boxes for the idols and staff or helping to promote a drama or a movie in which the idols appear.

Example)
Fans created a *support* event where they handed out promotional flyers about their biases' upcoming show.

탈락 Tal Lak
(t'al-lak)

Noun. "Elimination"
A term frequently used in competitive games or TV shows (i.e., quiz shows or audition programs).

Example)
Ok, the results are in… Jenny, you are *tal lak*!

Talent

Noun. "Drama Actor/Actress"
A drama (soap opera) actor/actress. Not used for a movie actor/actress.

Example)
Inhye: He looks amazing! Is he a movie star?
Yong: Nah, he is a *talent*. He appeared on the drama 'Forever You'.

팀킬 Team Kill

Noun. "Friendly Fire"
Originated from FPS (first-person shooter) games where a player mistakenly shoots and kills a team member. In real life settings, it refers to someone saying/doing things that cause harm to their own group.
Example)
Kong: Juno just spilled the beans on TV. He said one of the group members likes wearing girls undies.
Chong: That is one hell of a *team kill*.

Teaser

Noun. "Sneak Preview"
Usually used by entertainment companies before a full release of an album/MV, done to build a buzz towards the release of the upcoming work.

Example)

Sexy Stars just released a 30-second-long *teaser* clip on YouTube before the full album release.

Teaser Pics

Noun. "Photos Released by Entertainment Companies Before Official Release"

The photos released by entertainment companies before the release of a song/album of an idol/group. They can be either solo shots or group shots incorporating the theme of their upcoming work.

Example)
XeeXee's *teaser pics* indicate that their next album will have being comical as their concept.

특종 Teuk Jong
(t'ŭk-jong)

Noun. "Exclusive Story", "Scoop"

Something all reporters and news agencies want every day, but something fanboys/girls don't, because most of them are related to something negative, such as their bias getting involved in a crime or the group's abrupt disbandment.

Example)
Mispatch just released another *teuk jong*! They say MR. & MS. are a married couple!

타이틀 트랙 Title Track

Noun. "Main Song of an Album"

The main promoted track in an album. This is the song that usually has an accompanying music video and is performed on music shows.

Example)

The *title track* for their new album is "Magical Moments", because it symbolizes their dramatic return as one group after disbanding last year.

Trainee

Noun.
Someone who goes through vigorous training with a dream to become a KPOP star one day. The training can last as long as 10+ years before they finally make a debut, but it is not a guarantee - entertainment companies have the right to release them if they believe their trainees don't have what it takes to become a KPOP star.

Example)
Before becoming a top star, John T was a *trainee* for 8 years.

Triple Crown

Noun. "Winning Three Weeks in a Row on One Music Show"
Winning three weeks in a row on one music show (e.g., Music Bank). It is NOT winning on three different shows (e.g., Music Bank, Inki Gayo, M!Countdown) the same week. Once achieved, the song is taken out of the running for #1.

Example)
Oppa's won last 2 weeks in a row! If Oppa's win again this week, they will achieve *triple crown*!

트로트 Trot
(t'ŭ-ro-t'ŭ)

Noun. "Old-fahsioned Korean Music Genre"
Commonly known as "뽕짝" *ppong jjak* due to its distinctive background rhythm, it is the oldest form of Korean pop music. Once considered a genre popular only among the old timers, but thanks to the efforts of contemporary musicians (e.g., Jang Yoon Jeong, Dae Sung), it has a considerable share of fan base among the younger generation as well.

Example)
Mira thought only old people like *trot*, but when she heard her bias sing it, she fell in love with it.

얼짱 Ulzzang (Uljjang)
(ŏl-tchang)

Noun. "The Best Looking"

Literally meaning "the best face", it is used to describe someone with good looks. Again, it's just the face that matters and nothing else, so even if you are overweight with a huge beer belly, you can still be an ulzzang if your face is pretty.

Example)
In my selca's I am an *ulzzang*, but when I take a full body shot I am an obese *ulzzang*.

엄친아/엄친딸 Umchin A / Umchin Ddal
(ŏm-ch'i-na/ŏm-ch'in-ttal)

Noun. "Golden Boy/Girl"

Literally meaning "Mom's friend's son/daughter". It is someone who is better than you in every aspect, to a degree that you doubt their existence. Often times it is an imaginary person your mom makes up to make a comparison with you, hoping to make you try harder.

Example)
Bobo graduated high school at 10, and college at 14. She makes tons of money as a business woman and can play 5 musical instruments. She is a real *umchina*.

엄마 Umma
(ŏm-ma)

Noun. "Mom"

Also something you say when startled, similar to saying "Oh my god!".

Example)
Umma! Dinner! I am hungry!

언니 Unnie
(ŏn-ni)

Noun. `"Older Female Sibling"`
A term which a female uses to address an older female sibling, but it can be used to address any older female with whom significant emotional intimacy is shared. It can also be used to address a waitress at a restaurant. It can be used in place of someone's name.

Example)
Unnie, what should we get for umma's birthday?

V Line

Noun. `"Sleek Jaw Line"`
The shape of a jaw line that resembles the alphabet V. It is a compliment because it symbolizes sleek jaw line which is an attribute associated with "small face".

Example)
After losing so much weight, I got my *V Line* back.

V.I.P

Noun. `"Official Big Bang Fan Club"`
It is named after a track on their second single. Members usually use either yellow crown light sticks or bandanas to "support". They were nominated as the "Best Fan" by MTV Italy TRL Awards in 2012.

Example)
Jenny: I am a *V.I.P*!
Hoang: What makes you so special?
Jenny: I mean I am a member of *V.I.P*! Big Bang's fan club!

Visual

Noun. "Looks"

A reference to one's appearance, usually the face.

Example)
Jaeho, the leader of the group Xtars, is also in charge of *visual*, because he is the best looking among all.
My *visual* is better than yours! I am so much more prettier.

비타민 Vitamin

Noun. "Life of the Party"

Also known as "happy virus", it refers to someone who brings good vibes to a group.
Example)
Marcus is the most positive person in the world. He is liked by everyone around him. That's why he earned the nick name of *vitamin*.

왜? Wae?
(wae)

Interjection. "Why?"

An expression used to confirm the validity of something. It is also something people say in K-Dramas and K-Movies after breaking up.

Example)
She dumped me. *Wae? Wae? Wae!*

완소 Wan So
(wan-so)

Adjective. "Most Cherished"

An abbreviation for "완전" *wan jeon* ("absolutely, completely") + "소중" *so joong* ("precious"). It is used in conjunction with other nouns (e.g., 완소 아템 *wan so atem* ("super rare item"), 완소남/녀 *wan so nam/neyo* ("most adorable man/lady"). Hence, simply adding it to another noun brings it to the superlative degree.

Example)
Mariah: I got a new iPhone! This is my new *wan so* item! I will cherish it forever!
Andrew: Forever? You mean 2 weeks, right?

왕따 Wang Dda
(wang-tta)

Noun. "Outcast"
Someone who has been rejected by society or by a social group, it most frequently occurs in school. It has become a serious social issue as young victims often choose to end their own lives.

Example)
Before debuting, Gosoo was a *wang dda* because his parents came from North Korea, but he was finally accepted as a vital part of the group.

화이트 데이 White Day

Noun. "The Day When Men Reciprocate the Gifts Received on Valentine's Day With Chocolate"
March 14, which is observed as a day when men to give women chocolate, either as a token of repayment for the gifts received on Valentine's Day, or to ask her out.

Example)
Didn't get anything from anyone on Valentine's Day, so don't have to give anyone anything on *White Day*, either,

월요병 Wol Yo Byeong
(wŏ-ryo-byŏng)

Noun. "The Monday Blues"
The drastic mood swing one experiences after the weekend. Symptoms include lethargy, a sense of hopelessness, and complete lack of motivation.

Example)
Wol yo byeong is the type of disease that you know is inevitable, and it hits you the worst after spending the weekend partying.

우결 Woo Gyeol
(u-gyŏl)

Noun. "Popular Reality Show by MBC"
Shrot for "우리 결혼했어요" *woori gyeolhon gaet eo yo* ("we got married"). It is a popular reality show where idols/celebs are paired up to expeirence what life would be like if they were married.

Example)
Tim: OMG! Jenna and Min are getting married!
Anna: WTH? No way! For real?
Tim: Nah… just in Woo Gyeol
Anna: Kkam nol!

움짤 Woom Jjal (Um Jjal)
(um-tchal)

Noun. "GIF"
An abbreviation for "움직이는" *woom jik i neun* ("animated") "짤방" *jjal bang* ("a photo that is attached to a forum thread to avoid automatic deletion by the system after being falsely flagged as an "empty thread"). In the KPOP realm, it is usually an animated short clip of idols making funny faces, bloopers, and dance moves (e.g., wave dance). It is similar to GIFs.

Example)
Holly: Why do people post irrelevant photos on their posts in this forum?
Jax: Oh, its called *woom jjal*. They have to stick it in there so the moderators don't assume that there is no contents inside.

World Star

Noun. "KPOP Celeb Who is Also Popular Outside of Asia"
The title given to a KPOP celeb who is also popular outside Asia.

Example)
May Kim's new song got to the Top 10 Billboard Chart. She is a *world star* now.

X Line

Noun. "Long, Skinny Legs Connected by a Slim Waist"
So termed becauses the shape is similar to the Latin letter X.

Example)
Gongmi's got such a model body. Look at her *X Line!*

야동 Ya Dong
(ya-dong)

Noun. "Porn Clips"
An abbreviation for "야한" *ya han* ("sexy") + "동영상" *dong yeong sang* ("movie clip"). They are often stored in a secret folder on a computer with a name that has nothing to do with its content, to discourage any unwanted third party access.

Example)
There are two types of men. 1 that watches *ya dong* and 1 that says they don't (liars!).

야! Ya!
(ya)

Interjection. "Hey!"
Used to grab someone's attention, but shouldn't be used to address someone older.

Example)
Jenna: *Ya!* Minho!
Mark: Hi, do I know you?
Jenna: Oh, I thought you were Minho. Sorry!

양다리 Yang Da Ri
(yang-da-ri)

Noun. "Two Timing Someone"
Literally means "two (double) legs" or "two (double) bridges" and is figuratively used to refer to cheating on your boyfriend/girlfriend.

Example)
Timmy got caught doing his *yang da ri*, and lost both girls.

예능 Ye Neung
(ye-nŭng)

Noun. "Entertainment"
A TV show genre (e.g., talk show, "variety" game show, etc.) that is less formal and fun-oriented than other programs (e.g., documentary, news, etc.). It is a great opportunity for the members of a group because they get a chance to show off their unique talents (e.g., impression, singing, dance moves, etc.) as individuals.

Example)
Everybody was surprised to see Mingoo on the *ye neung* TV show last night because he was thought to be a really quiet person.

예헷 Yehet
(ye-het)

Interjection. "All Right"
The sound Oh Sehun, a member of EXO makes to express joy and satisfaction.

Example)
I finished my homework! *Yehet!*

여보 Yeo bo
(yŏ-bo)

Noun. "Sweetheart"
A term which a married couple uses to address each other.

Example)
I am going to marry Yugyu Oppa! He will be my *Yeobo!* Sa Rang Hae~!

여보세요 Yeo Bo Se Yo
(yŏ-bo-se-yo)

Phrase. "Hello (on the phone)" "Excuse Me (trying to grab someone's attention)"
Believed to be made up of words "여기" *yeogi* ("here") + "보세요" *bo se yo* ("please look") = "please look here".

Example)
Bubba: *Yeo bo se yo?* Is Mary home?
Wonkyu: Mary? Who's Mary?
Bubba: Oops! Wrong number, sorry!

열도 Yeol Do
(yŏl-do)

Noun. "Japan"
An Internet term mostly used by the younger generation of Korean netizens. Literally means "archipelago", which is the type of landform Japan has, and since there aren't very many countries that are archipelagos, netizens simply use it to refer to Japan. It is most frequently used in the form of "열도의" *yeol do eui* ~sth = "sth of Japan". For example, "열도의 발명품 *bal myeong poom* ("invention")" is "Japan's invention".

Example)
Yeol do has their own thing, called JPOP, and it offers different flavors than KPOP.

열공 Yeol Gong
(yŏl-gong)

Noun. "SMAO (Studying My Ass Off)"
An abbreviation for "열심히" *yeol shim hi* ("hard, zealously") + "공부"
gong boo ("study") = "studying really hard".

Example)
Kid: Good students' anthem! Enjoy your bool geum and nol to, and *yeol gong*!

열정페이 Yeol Jeong Pay
(yŏl-chŏng-p'e-i)

Noun. "Employers Exploiting Young Labor"
Literal meaning is "passion pay", originated as tongue-in-cheek satire to criticize vicious employers who exploit young employees. Most of the victims are often interns who feel fortunate to even have an opportunity due to the difficult employment conditions in Korea. Knowing this, employers choose to pay very little or nothing for the employee's contribution. They rationalize such an act by arguing that they should work with passion and not for money, as they are learning valuable lessons for free.

Example)
Many young Korean job seekers believe that *yeol jeong pay* should be vanished from this world.

열폭 Yeol Pok
(yŏl-p'ok)

Noun. "Inferiority Complex"
An abbreviation for "열등감 *yeol deung gam* (feeling inferior) + 폭발 *pok bal* (explosion, rupture) = "jealousy/inferiority explosion". It means acting rude or hostile towards someone, out of a sense of inferiority.

Example)
Ronda: Ha, did you see Jenny's new dress? I bet she stole it from the

store. Look at her hair! I am sure she's wearing a wig.
Darren: Dude… You are just having a *yeol pok*…

연습 Yeon Seup
(yŏn-sŭp)

Noun. `"Training"`
Something an aspiring KPOP idol must go through before making an
official debut, usually involving singing, dancing, and even acting training,
depending on one's talent.

Example)
Through 7 years of hard *yeon seup* as a training, Zex finally debuted.

연예인 Yeon Ye In
(yŏ-nye-in)

Noun. `"Entertainer"`
An "entertainer", it can also be used to refer to someone who is publicly
well-known (i.e., a "celeb").

Example)
These days, kids' number one dream is to become a famous *yeon ye in*.

용꿈 Yong Ggum
(yong-kkum)

Noun. `"Good Omen"`
Mainly because the dragon is considered a holy animal in Korean culture.
Hence, seeing it in your dream is thought to be a sure sign of good fortune
coming your way; many Koreans would head straight to buy a lottery
ticket.

Example)
Wally bought lottery tickets after seeing G-Dragon, hoping it would count
as a *yong ggum*.

유혹 Yoo Hok
(yu-hok)

Noun. "Seduction"
The mother of all problems. In K-Dramas, when "love lines" become tangled up.

Example)
Guys who fall for *yoo h*ok can lose many things.

ㄱ ㄱ

Chat Acronym. "Hurry", "Let's Go"
An acronym created by taking the initial consonants of the word "고고" (*go go*). It gained popularity as e-sports players started using it, when they had to type bursts of short messages to push the game moderator to start the game. The more you type the word, the more powerful the message becomes. It should not be used with someone who is older or who has no sense of closeness with you yet.
Example)
(Text from teacher) Ok, guys! Are we ready for a field trip?
(Text from students) ㄱ ㄱ ㄱ ㄱ ㄱ ㄱ ㄱ ㄱ ㄱ ㄱ ㄱ

ㄱ ㅅ

Chat Acronym. "Thx"
An acronym created by taking the initial consonants of the word " 감사" *gamsa* ("appreciation"). Although it is a formal way of expressing gratitude, the abbreviated form must only be used to address someone very close (i.e., friends), as it might seem disrespectful otherwise.

Example)
(Text from mom) Your lunch is in the fridge.
(Text from daugther) ㄱ ㅅ

ㄴㄴ

Chat Acronym. "No No"

An acronym created by taking the initial consonants of the word "노노" no no. It is used to express disagreement or rejection. It is also synonymous with "안돼 and wae. It, should not be used with someone who is older or who has no sense of closeness with you yet.

Example)
(Text from Jenny) Hey, wanna go hit the movies?
(Text from Mark) ㄴㄴ. Gotta study.

ㄷㄷ

Chat Acronym. "Shivering"

An acronym created by taking the initial consonants of the word "덜덜" deol deolan, an adjective describing the act of shivering, caused by either cold or fear.

Example)
(Text from Suzi) Hey, your boyfriend found out about what you did last night.
(Text from Jane) ㄷㄷ

ㅂㄷㅂㄷ

Chat Acronym. "Trembling with Rage"

An acronym created by taking the initial consonants of the word "부들부들" boo deul boo deul. Not to be confused with ㅎㄴㄴ ("shivering"), which is your body's reaction to cold or fear.

Example)
(Text from Hanna) Yo! I just finished the last hot dog!
(Text from Mitchelle) ㅂㄷㅂㄷ

ㅅ ㄱ

Chat Acronym. `"Peace Out"`
An acronym created by taking the initial consonants of the word "수고" *soo go* ("trouble"/"effort"). Aside from its literal meaning, it is used as a way of saying goodbye, especially in workplace settings. For example, "수고 하세요" *soo go haseyo* can be translated as "keep up the good work". The abbreviated form, "수고" and its acronym "ㅅ ㄱ", however, should never be said in formal settings.

Example)
(Text from Tim) All right dawg, peace out!
(Text from Ori) ㅅ ㄱ!

ㅅ ㅂ

Chat Acronym. `"F***", "SHI*"`
An acronym created by taking the initial consonants of the word "시(씨)발" *si bal* ("f***" or "s***"). It is most frequently used to put a strong emphasis on something you say, or as a natural response to a startling situation. It, should not be used with someone who is older or who has no sense of closeness with you yet.

Example)
(Text from Brad) ㅅ ㅂ! I forgot to do my homework!
(Text from Jen) You are in big trouble!

ㅇ ㅇ

Chat Acronym. `"k"`
An acronym created by taking the initial consonants of the word "응응" *eung eung* ("yes yes"). It is used to express agreement or acknowledgment in a conversation. It, should not be used with someone who is older or who has no sense of closeness with you yet.

Example)
(Text from Sera) Did you have lunch?
(Text from Mark) ㅇ ㅇ

ㅇ ㅈ

Chat Acronym. "ACK"

An acronym created by taking the initial consonants of the word "인정" *in jeong* ("acknowledgment"). It is used to express agreement or approval. It should not be used with someone who is older or who has no sense of closeness with you yet.

Example)
(Text from Brian) Don't you think our gym teacher is too fat to be a good role model?
(Text from Amy) ㅇ ㅈ

ㅈ ㅅ

Chat Acronym. "SRY"

An acronym made up by taking the initial consonants of the word "죄송" *joe song* ("sorry, my fault, regrets"). Do not use this abbreviation in a serious situation as it might seem insincere.

Example)
(Text from Wonmi) Hey! Did you spill coffee on my notebook?
(Text from Pam) ㅈ ㅅ!

ㅊ ㅋ ㅊ ㅋ

Phrase. "Congrats"

An acronym created by taking the initial consonants of the word "추카추카", a colloquial version of "축하축하" *chook ha chook ha* ("congrats, congrats"), but it should never be used with someone older as it is considered rude. You should use the formal version "축하합니다" *chook ha hap ni da.*

Example)
George got fired after sending his boss ㅊ ㅋ ㅊ ㅋ for her birthday.

ㅋㅋㅋ

Chat Acronym. "LOL"
Text used to express amusement.

Example)
When I chat with him, he is so funny that I can say nothing but ㅋㅋㅋ.

K-POP
Conversation

Joey: *Otoke!* I am so late to *alba...*!
Mom: Joey, *jebal* try to wake up early, okay? *Jebal!*

Youngho: *Hyung,* can I please use your iPad?
Moongyu: Hey my little *dong saeng*, you should call me *hyungnim*. I am your big brother!
Youngho: Okay... what can I do? You are the *gab* and I am the *eul* here...
Moongyu: Okay buddy, here you go. Have fun!
Youngho: *Gomawo!*

Kayla: *Omo!* At this rate, I am going to miss my Oppa's *gong yeon!*
Tiffany: *Gwenchana!* The watch gains time. We still have 10 minutes.

Michael: *Jagi,* I have a confession to make.
Sonya: What is it? You are making me *gin jang...* my palms are sweaty!
Michael: I've got 2 tickets to *Golden Disk Awards!*
Sonya: *Daebak!* That is so fantastic! Honey you are the best!

Bouncer: Can I see your ID please?
Wonju: Here you go, sir.
Bouncer: Dang, you are 30? You are doing so well for your age. What a *dong an* you have.
Wonju: LOL but check out my *D Line* I got from drinking so much beer. It tells my real age.

Choa: Oppa's won *Gaon Chart, Gayo Daejeon, Music Bank, Inki Gayo...* they are on the way to *all-killing* the charts!
Pamela: *Cheongmal?* I wonder what the *antis* would say about this! They will get so jealous.

Gyuho: My summer goal: Lose 30 pounds and get *S Line* body and *X Line* body!
John: *Wae?* You look just fine now.
Gyuho: No, I look like an *ajumma* now... My *V Line* has gone missing for quite a long time...

Mellow Girls' new *concept* provoked so many fans, which resulted in expressing their discontent through creating *black ocean* at concerts.

It's been 3 months since my hyung went to the army… Aww… *bogoshipo…!* Oh, no homo. This is just a *bromance*.

Tin Tin's new *digital single* is available for download online, but it's too bad I can't see their new *choom* on TV until next month. They are the best *dance-dols.*
JYP Nation, SM, and YG Entertainment all sent their best idol groups to the *Dream Concert,* causing massive *fan wars* between 12 *fan clubs.*.

Tal Lak? Or *Hap Gyuk?* It depends on how much *Inki* a candidate has!

Hul… this drama has a really twisted *love line…* Isn't this a pure *makjang* drama? All the *baewoo's* need to improve their acting skills as well!

Ajusshi: Ya! I am 20 years older than you. Don't you dare talk to me in *banmal.* Use *Jon Dae Mal*!
Fei Fei: Oh, *mianhae*! I am from Hong Kong!
Ajusshi: Oh, I am sorry! I understand! Your Korean is really good! *Jjang!*
Fei Fei: *Kamsa Hamnida!*

Mwong mi? you love Korean food but can't eat *Kimchi? Mi Chyeo Sso?* You should give it a try! It is really *mashisso~!*

Answer my question using *nae or aniyo* only!

I am really looking forward to *Chuseok* where I get 5 days off! I will be chilling in *Gangnam* maybe wearing *Hanbok.*

If a *gamdok* says *NG,* you have to start over. That's why you need a lot of acting *yeon seup*!

Aegyo is the biggest weapon a girl can have… but *age line* is their worst enemy!

Aegyo Sal can make a girl's eyes look bigger, but if an *ajusshi* does it, a*igoo,* I don't even want to think about it… *andwae!*

Apa… my *maum apa* because my Oppa is going to the *Army.* I will wait for his *come back stage* no matter how long it takes…

Eww, Mark looks so *ssanti* dancing only in his underwear! He looks like a *byuntae!*

Yohee: Jaime's got a *casting* for a new *CF*! He will be acting as a rich *chaebol.*
Mina: *Chincha?* Will he show off his *chocolate abs?*
Yohee: I really hope so, I just hope he doesn't do anything *choding* that makes him look like a little kid.

Max: Oh my god, I drank 5 cartons of *banana milk*… My stomach is going to explode!
Wilson: *Babo!*
Max: Q_Q

Only a *gwiyomi* should do the *bbuing bbuing* and only a *bagel girl/ boy* should do the *.bodyrolls*

All the trainees at the *Big 3* dream of becoming a *world star* one day.

Hyunhwa used to be my *bias*, only until I saw Miho, a true *bias ruiner* with her seductive *eye smile.*

Yong: Jenny, you have such a beautiful face! Did you get that *visual* from your *eomeoni?*
Jenny: Nope, from *plastic surgery.*

Gangnam Style is a prime example of how *Hallyu* can impact the people around the globe! They can't even understand the *gasa*.

Time to say goodbye! *Hang Syo!*

Honey thighs can be achieved through vigorous leg exercises and proper diet.

I used to be an *ulzzang* thanks to my beautiful face and a *queenka* thanks to my rich dad. Combined together, I was a real *umchinddal!*

Because I *sa rang hae* my Oppa's so much, I broke into their *jib*, only to realize I became a *stan*, or even a *saseng!*

When taking pictures with his fans, he does *manner hands* and *manner legs*. He is so considerate!

My parents set up a *mat seon* for me… To my surprise, he was a real *hoon nam* of my style. Guess what? We are in *Jeju Island* now haha. People call us *Mi Nam & Mi Nyeo* couple. Believe it or not.

Men bung is the word you used when your Oppa falls to his knees while giving you a *piggy back*.

If I can be a *talent*, I will do anything, including at the cost of being called a *plastic prince*.

Whenever I am stressed out, I hit the *pojangmacha* near my office and drink *soju* with my friends, followed by an intensive *noraebang* session.

Have you lost weight? You got such a *small face* now. I didn't know you had a *V Line*!

I am not sure if I am his girlfriend or just a *some nyeo*.

That drama would have been so boring without that *ballad OST.*

As a *fashionista* and a *hoon nam*, I deserved the right to be the leader of the *fan club!*

Jeez, the game is about to start... Oppa's *fighting!*

Her *min nat* is better than with make up on.

Taemin, the *maknae* of the group UOU, is a *noona killer* who has the potential of turning a normal *noona* into a *pedo noona* by igniting a *noona romance* with his *flower boy* face.

The reason the song became such a popular song is not because it was a *hook song* but because his *mok so ri* was so sweet.

Yeonhee: *Unnie,* come take a *selca* with me~!
Myong: *Shiro!* I look terrible now. Let's do it *naeil.*
Yeonhee: No~ *onul!* You look just fine! You are no You are no *yeon ye in* why do you care so much about your looks?

Oppa's who are great at *fan service* reacts to *fan chants*, reads the *fan fiction* written by the fans, and doesn't get involved in any ugly *scandals.*

I look great! All the countless hours I spent at the gym is finally paying off! I am a *momzzang! Yehet!*

A: You talk too much... the only way to make you *a dak* is by putting food in your mouth!
B: Oh, so we are going out for *a jeom*? What are we having?

A: *A nwa...!* I lost my valuable *a tem*!
B: You *ae ja*! You paid $100 for that thing!

A: I wish I had an *ae-in*... I'm so lonely!
B: You might want to consider ditching that *ajae* hair style then.

A: Hahaha! I am the most notorious for writing *ak peul*'s on peoples posts!

B: Um… *an mool an goong*!

A: I failed the test again… *an seup*… and to make it worse, I am *bae go pa*!

A: My opinion on you going out with that dude is *ban dae*! He was in *ban mo* the first time we met, without my permission.

A: The worst kind of *bbeol geul* I wrote was when I pretended like a real idol, but it was all *bbeong*!

A: Dude! Buy that car! It will be so *bbo dae*!

B: Are you *bbom bbu*ing me?

A: Are you my *be peu?* If so, can you please *beo ca choong* for me at the next *beo jeong*?

A: Hey, do you think I can have James as my *bi chin?*

B: Nope, *bi choo*! He's got a big mouth!

A: I am so handsome~ I am the B*i (Vi) dam* of this town~ everybody would fall in love with me at first sight~ but if not, you eventually will cause I am also a *bol mae~*!

A: Turn on the TV! Time to *bon bang sa soo*!

A: Damn, somebody *bool peom*'ed our private *bool geum* photos! So embarrassing!

A: My bias was *buffering* on stage because he forgot his line… I think he wanted to *burrow*…

A: Hot damn! What's with your ugly hairdo? It's so *byeong mat*!

A: In the army, they do a *chool chek* in *da na ka* style.

A: Yay! I *deuk tem*'ed that girl's photo!

B: Dude! That's called *do chwal*!

A: Brian asked her why she became a *dol sing*. That was one *dol jik goo*…

A: I heard Yong is such a *deok hoo*, that he sleeps with a cardboard cut out of a game character lol!
B: Well that's kind of a *dwit book* because he now has a real girlfriend.

A: My profile photo is a huge *ek bak*… I don't now how to fix it!
B: Don't fix it. It's way better than your *eol bbang* face.

A: Hello, *eoseo oseyo* to our restaurant!
B: Meh, I changed my mind. I'll come next time.
A: No, *ga ji ma*!

A: Don't make fun of me for rinsing my Kimchi it is a *gae chwi*! As a matter of fact, I *gang choo* you doing it because it is not too hot. Of course, it would look less *ganji*.

A: That new guy is my *gasip nam*…
B: What? *Geo jit mal*… You said I was the one!

A: Jenny singlehandedly beat 3 thugs… *God*-Jenny!

A: Ughhh! When are the oppa's going to make a come back? It's been over a year and became a *gogooma*!
B: They just announced it on their *gong home*!

A: Honey, I am not *goong ye*, but thought you would like this ring!
B: Awww… you are so thoughtful! Come here *goongdi pang pang*!

A: She dresses up like a whore because she is just a *gwan jong*…
B: Maybe she is just too lazy? Heard she practicies *gwichanism*.

A: He turned out to be a *heo jeob* with *heuk soo jeo*… And the reason why he's so broke is he spends all his money doing *hyeon jil*. I still *i bool kick* that I once thought he was cute.

A: Someone posted in *ik ge* that you were a high school *il jin*…
Man, you going down…

A: Dude! You might want to *ja sak* the post… It's been mentioned so many times already. It's a *jae bang song*!

A: You are not funny. No *jam*!

B: *Jeul*! That's what I wanted to say!

A: I bought this new car because of *ji reum shin* told me to do so!

A: Damn, is that a *jik jjik* of M-Dragon at a club? Wait… it is a total *jja ga*! It's all *Po Shop*'ed! You are a *jji jil i* and you should know that lol.

A: Would people thnk that I am *jon ye*?
B: *Ke ba ke* and *sa ba sa*, but I think you are.
A: Thank you! You are *king wang jjang*!

A: *Kkam nol*! What are you doing here at *kong da bang*? You don't even drink coffee!
B: I am just enjoying my break, reminiscing about good old memories during my *leeds si jeol*.
A: Dude… everybody knows you were just a *meok twi* who got a huge signing bonus through a well-played *mil dang*!

A: Hey girl, *nae ge ro wa*!
B: Nope, I already have a *nam chin*.
A: Whaaaa…? I thought he was just a *nam sa chingoo*!
B: We are dating and he is so much better than you in every way. He is a real *neom sa byeok* to you!

A: LOL I wrote a *naeng moo* e-mail with the title "urgent" to *nak si* my colleague at work.

A: I heard that *new pe* at work is a *noe sake nam,* but he is just a *newbie* to me. I will teach him who the alpha male is.
B: LOL you say that every time there is a *new pe*. You sound like a *nok hwa bang song*.

A: Hey *old miss*! I am not interested in you. You are *out of an joong*, so don't you be a *ping peu* and order me around through Kakao talk!
B: What? When did I do that?
A: Right here! Look at this *seu shot* of you ordering me to do things!

A: I shouldn't believe any of the girls' photos online because of *po shop*...

A: I am a *oom jeol nam*!
B: *Rae al*? Who is the lucky girl?
A: A *se jel ye*!
B: This is such a *sa i da* news! I thought you would never find one! Congrats!
A: Oh, I have to add that her *saeng eol* is not *se jel ye*, though.

A: Honey, your *sha bang sha bang* beauty literally made my heart go *shim koong*!

A: Honey, do you like my *sin sang* dress? It's my new *wan so* dress!
B: *Ye obo se you*, are you out of your mind? We have less than $100 in our bank! This is a *team kill*! Ugh... I shouldn't have *sokdo wiban*'ed and married someone else... *OTL*.
A: How can you say that! *Ssa ga ji*!
B: Never mind. I am smiling~
A: That's the ugliest *sseok so* I've ever seen.

(In a group chat)

A: ㄱㄱ !!
B: ㄴㄴ !!

A: Why not? My parents will be here any minute ㄷㄷ ... Let's play just one more round!

C: Well, mine are here. Gotta go! ㅅㄱ !
A: ㅅㅂ ... I guess it's just you and me then!
B: ㅇㅇ

A: Hold up. Let me go have a quick *DB*.

A: Are my jokes outdated? My kids call them *ajae gag*.
B: I think it's *bok bool bok*, and depends on the person.

A: Our oppa's new *an moo* is so difficult to follow.
B: *Assa!* I just mastered all the moves!
A: Our oppa's *bal yeon gi* makes him look like an idiot. *sigh*
B: But he still has the best face in *ban do*. He should be forgiven.

A: Did you send your common sense to the *Andromeda*? You can't *boo bi boo bi* me, I am your sister!
B: Ugh! Don't be a *drama queen*! I barely touched you!

A: *Cheol byeok nyeo*'s often have a difficult time finding their ideal man.
B: Yup, that's why your sister's eating jjajang myun on upcoming *black day.*

A: *Cheol sae fans* have no loyalty or whatsoever!
B: I disagree. It's not like you only have to love your *cheot sa rang* forever and ever!

A: *Chi maek* is a *colabo* between chicken and beer.
B: LOL! That was a funny *drib*.

A: Not sure he really likes me or doing *eo jang gwan ri* with me…
B: One way to find out! *Dash!*

A: My oppa is a *ye neung chobo*. He has never been on a variety TV show before.
B: I hope he can blend in with all the *ddo ra i* comedians!

A: As a *homo intern*s, I agree that the only type of compensation I receive is *dda bong*, because it is my *yeol jeong pay*.
B: Those employers are really *moo gae nyeon*… They have no compassion.

A: Oh! A bikini pic! *Gaen so!*

B: I even have a *fan cam* version of it. Want to trade?

A: I became *geup* happy when I heard our oppa's comeback announcement.

B: I read that *gisa* too! It is a *gong sik* announcement!

A: Our oppa's are having a *guerilla concert*! Let's go *eung won*! Go grab our *slogans*!

B: *Ona jeon* happy! My *yong ggum* last night really must have meant something good!

A: *OME! OME!* Is that *ya dong* you are watching?

B: Come on, enough with your *oh ji rap!* Just respect my privacy would you? Oh who am I kidding. You have no *noon chi*.

A: What is *White Day*? I know *Black Day* becuase I am a *motae solo...*

B: But everybody loves you! You are such a *vitamin* who bring joy to he group.

A: After getting a *ssang soo,* Mary became a whole new girl! She is so *sha bang sha bang* now.

B: *Sol kka mal*, her eyes do look fake to me.

A: Can my fan club activities be included as a *spec* on the resume?

B: Why don't you pass the *soo neung* first?

A: *Maldo andwae...* You just finished that *kim ddeok soon*? I thought you were on a diet? That's like 3,000 calories!

B: I know... My *shik shin* instinct got the better of me...

A: I love my *in gang* courses. I learn so much from them.

B: You know that they are *molca's* from classrooms?

A: The new member of the group became a *wang dda* after not giving *in sa* to his senior members.

B: What a *maeng gu...* It sounds like they will make a *kong ga ru* group...

A: *Dispatch* released another *teuk jong*! QUQU got caught doing *jak eop* on a girl.

B: *Haek* surprise! I thought she had a girlfriend already!

A: Did you know that *dda bong* and *jo a yo* mean the same?

B: *Hyeon woot*, man! You must be the only person in the world who didn't know that.

A: In *hell Joseon*, there is no such thing as *kal twae*. You have to work, work, and work.

B: It sounds like a *noye gye yak* to me.

A: Did you know that Martha used to be an *oh jing eo*h before the plastic surgery?

B: Yup, I *Naverd* it and saw the pictures. Definitely not *my style*.

A: The movie became a big hit thanks to the heroin's *mi jon*. She really is *man leb* at acting.

B: Yup, she is a *gosu* actor, the master.

A: Bbuing~ Bbuing~

B: What's with that *gwi cheok*? I want to throw up!

A: My *in ji do* is so low even in my family that my mom often forgets my name.

B: I heard you didn't get a *saeng seon* on your birthday, either!

A: Our oppa's new *title track* is a *trot* song!

B: That will make my parents *ip deok* as well!

A: The biggest *jin sang* when drinking is someone who forces you to be a *heuk gi sa* for her.

B: Yeah! They are a prime example of *dap jeong neo*!

A: I invited everybody to the dan tok, and later found out that I accidentally included my boss…

B: It's a disaster waiting to happen.

A: According to my *gam*, that couple will break up in the final episode!
B: You just watched *joo jang mi*, didn't you?

A: Oh yeah~ *Assa*! My girlfriend gave these on *Pepero Day*!
B: Hey, don't be such a *pal bool chool* and be courteous of others who don't have a girlfriend.

A: Oppa's going to *showcase* his *shin gok* on TV!
B: We should throw a *support* event!

A: Oppa's new music video was made all *locae* in Brazil!
B: I bet he got many *love calls* from the showbiz people there!

A: Oppa's got a *sak bal* for the army ;(
B: But he still looks so handsome <3

A: Jenny, the *keyboard warrior*, got a *go so mi* for leaving tens of thousands of malicious comments on her *SNS*!
B: We have to make sure that she doesn't show up at the *sign hwae*.

A: Johhny got pulled over and kept claiming that he didn't drink a single drop of alcohol, but the officer found 5 bottles of empty beer cans in the passenger seat. It was a *bbae bak* moment for Johnny.

A: All of a sudden, I have zero energy and motivation.
B: That's because it's Monday today. I'm afraid you are diagnosed with *wol yo byeong*.

A: What is your *wanso* item?
B: My oppa's debut CD. I won't trade it for anything.

A: I've been seeing this girl for 2 months, but she wouldn't even let me hold her hand. She is such a *cheol byeok nyeo*!
B: Try drinking *soju* with her. That ought to soften things up and you might get some *skinship* with her.

A: Oh my, my...! You are so drunk! Here, I will give you *eo boo ba*! Oh no... you just broke my back.

A: You are so pretty. You are *se jel ye*. I am blinded by your *sha bang sha bang* beauty!
B: You are such a sweet talker... I think you are a *seon soo!*

A: My oppa farted on the show and I bet everyone heard that...
B: Oh no... Too bad it wasn't a *nok hwa bang song.*

Kamsa Hapnida!

48737328R00113

Made in the USA
Middletown, DE
26 September 2017